20 Questions to Ask *About* Wills & Estates

Robert Zafft, Esq. and Gene Zafft, Esq.

CAREER
PRESS

THE CAREER PRESS, INC.
Franklin Lakes, NJ

20 QUESTIONS TO ASK ABOUT WILLS AND ESTATES
EDITED AND TYPESET BY KATE HENCHES
Cover design by Lu Rossman/Digi Dog Design
Printed in the U.S.A. by Book-mart Press

To order this title, please call toll-free 1-800-CAREER-1 (NJ and Canada: 201-848-0310) to order using VISA or MasterCard, or for further information on books from Career Press.

The Career Press, Inc., 3 Tice Road, PO Box 687,
Franklin Lakes, NJ 07417
www.careerpress.com

Library of Congress Cataloging-in-Publication Data

Zafft, Gene.
   20 questions to ask about wills and estates / Gene Zafft, Robert Zafft.
      p. cm.
   ISBN 1-56414-853-X (paper)
      1. Wills—United States—Miscellanea. 2. Estate planning—United States—Miscellanea. I. Title: Twenty questions to ask about wills and estates. II. Zafft, Robert. III. Title.

KF755.Z9Z34 2006
346.7305′6—dc22

2005045697

Dedication

To our wives,
Marlene and Tara Zafft

Contents

Introduction

Think what would happen if the breadwinner(s) in your family died suddenly. How well has the family's well-being and financial security been provided for? How much has been left to chance?

If you fell into an irreversible coma, would your family members know what your wishes were? Would they have the authority to act on these wishes, or would they face years of ruinous litigation while your body wasted away, connected to a feeding tube?

This book will help you and your loved ones expect—and plan for—the unexpected. You will learn how to use Wills and Estate planning to preserve and pass on wealth to loved ones, to make the most of insurance and retirement benefits, to minimize taxes, and to promote family welfare and harmony. In short, you will learn how to face whatever the future brings with confidence.

Peace of mind comes from being prepared. This book will show you how.

Question 1

What Happens if I Die Without a Will?

Live with passion, but die with a Will.
—Robert and Gene Zafft

What Is a Last Will and Testament?

A Last Will and Testament ("Will") is a document that sets forth a person's wishes with regard to:

- ⊃ the disposal of his or her physical remains
- ⊃ the distribution of his or her property (called the "Estate")
- ⊃ the care of persons for whom he or she had responsibility (such as minor children)

Even if drafted by another person (such as a lawyer), a Will is written in the first-person singular—the "I" voice. So, a typical Will might begin, "I, John Smith, being of sound mind and body,..."

A Will has to be signed by the person making it. Traditionally, the signing of the Will had to be witnessed by at least two adults. These adults could not be named as beneficiaries in the Will (that is, they could not receive any money or property from the Will).

The rules surrounding the making of a Will may seem old-fashioned, but they serve certain key purposes that hold true today. These are to help prove that:

13

1. the Will was actually signed by the person's whose name is on it

2. the maker of the Will was in his or her right mind when he or she signed it

3. he or she was not forced to sign it against his or her will

4. the Will was signed on a certain date, so that it can be determined whether the Will in question is, in fact, the last Will, or an earlier version that has been superseded by a later one

5. the Will was signed in a certain place, so that it can be determined whether all of the requirements for the making of a Will have been met under the laws of the place where it was signed.

This last point is worth repeating: a document that fails to satisfy *all* of the requirements for a Will is *not* a Will. You can revoke, amend, or replace your Will until the moment you die. But, if you die leaving behind a document you thought was a Will but isn't, your lawyer can't go to your plot in the cemetery to get a new one signed. If you want your final wishes to be respected and enforced, you have to do things right.

> *A document that fails to satisfy* all *the requirements for a Will is* not *a Will.*

A Word of Caution and a Suggestion

State law governs the making of Wills and what happens if you are considered to have died without a Will (because you never tried to make one or because the document you signed failed to qualify).

The basic rules that apply in this situation follow, but bear in mind that these rules vary from state to state and may change through time within any one state. Our goal in discussing them is to give you a general picture of what happens should you die without a Will.

The risks of making a mistake, however, do lead to one practical suggestion. Where a lawyer has drafted your Will, have that lawyer sign as a witness. Should a problem later arise with the document, the lawyer, having witnessed it, will prevent him or her from claiming that you signed without his knowledge or against his advice. This won't undo a mistake, but it may make it easier for your Estate or those hurt by your lawyer's error to prove he or she committed malpractice.

What Law Applies?

Generally, whether a document qualifies as a Will is determined by the law of the state in which the document was signed, even if the maker of the Will (the "Testator") later moves to another state. Where it is determined that no Will exists, the disposal of remains, distribution of property, and care of persons previously under the responsibility of the deceased will usually be determined by the law of the state where the person was residing at the time of death.

Management of Property Before It Is Distributed to Your Heirs

When you die, your property falls under the jurisdiction of a Probate Court (discussed in Question 2). If you die without a Will, the court will appoint an Administrator to locate and take charge of all of your assets, to pay your debts, and to manage your property until it is distributed to your heirs.

The Administrator will be entitled to fees for his or her work, which will be paid from your Estate. Your Estate will also have to pay any relevant attorney fees and court costs.

Control over the Estate and the right to collect this fee often give rise to competition and litigation among family members for appointment as Administrator.

Distribution of Property

Each State has adopted very precise laws of Descent and Distribution. Generally speaking, if a person without a Will dies:

➲ *unmarried and childless*, his or her property is divided equally among his or her parents and siblings.

➲ *married but without children*, some states give everything to the surviving spouse, while other states give the surviving spouse half, with the other half shared equally among the decedent's parents and/or siblings. (Where a sibling has died before his or her brother or sister, that sibling's descendants will divide whatever share of the property would have been distributed to the sibling.)

➲ *married with children*, usually the surviving spouse will get 1/2, while the children (or their descendants) divide the other half. In some states, however, the surviving spouse and his or her children are all treated the same and divide the entire estate equally among themselves. (Where a child has died before his or her parent, that child's descendants will divide whatever share of the property would have been distributed to the child.)

The absence of a Will precludes a person from excluding any of the previously mentioned relatives from sharing in an inheritance. With high incidents of divorce and remarriage, complicated relationships can arise among stepchildren, half-siblings, and so on, with bickering over who is entitled to how much. These situations represent land mines for litigation.

Guardianship of Minor Children and Property Left to Them

When a person with children dies, the surviving parent (whether a spouse or ex-spouse) becomes the sole Guardian. Sole Guardianship arises whether or not the decedent left a Will.

Where a couple with minor children die in a common disaster, such as a car accident or plane crash, and neither parent has left a Will appointing a Guardian, the court will give custody of the children to the closest relatives best able to care for them. In practice, frequent (and ugly) Guardianship battles arise between and among the maternal and paternal grandparents.

> *The absence of a Will precludes a person from excluding any of the previously mentioned relatives from sharing in an inheritance.*

Battles can also arise over the management of property left for the benefit of these children. In the absence of a Will (or Trust), the Guardian will have control, subject to court supervision, of any property left for the children's benefit. The Guardian will be entitled to fees for his or her services.

The supervision of the courts inevitably leads to attorney fees and court costs. Even seemingly commonplace expenses such as summer camp fees, health insurance, and braces for teeth can require the Guardian to apply for court permission.

Once a child reaches a certain age, usually 18 to 21, that child will be entitled to full control over his or her share of the property, whether or not he or she is mature enough to manage it well.

What happens if you die without a Will? Trouble, usually.

Q*uestion 2*

What Is Probate and How Much Time and Money Does It Take?

Talk is cheap, unless you're speaking with a lawyer.
—Robert Zafft

Some Basic Definitions

Probate is the legal procedure whereby a deceased person's assets (called his "Estate") are assembled, his debts determined and paid, and the net Estate (assets minus debts) distributed to his or her heirs. Probate is never speedy, but where the Decedent has left a properly drafted Will, the process should be relatively smooth and hassle free.

If the deceased person (called the "Decedent") dies without a Will, he is deemed to have died "Intestate." In such case, his Estate will be administered by a court-appointed Administrator.

If the Decedent left a Will, the decedent is deemed to have died "Testate" and is referred to as the "Testator." In almost all cases, the Will will name a "Personal Representative," or "Executor," to administer the Estate.

To sum up:

If there was not a Will:	If there was a Will:
Intestate	Testate/Testator
Court-appointed Administrator	Personal Representative or Executor named in the Will

Probate proceedings take place in the County where the decedent was residing at the time of death. Such proceedings take place in "Probate Court, " also called "Surrogate Court" in some states.

The Probate Court is usually a special division of the court system of each state. Special laws apply to its operations. As a rule, a Probate Judge hears matters without a jury.

Starting the Process

If the Decedent dies, or the Will fails to name a Personal Representative (Executor), a relative of the Decedent will usually start the probate process by applying to the Probate Court. If the Decedent's Will names an Executor, the Executor will usually make this application.

The application must be in writing, typically using forms approved by the Court. Where there is no Executor, an attorney often fills out the application, which is then signed by a relative of the Decedent. Filing fees vary from state to state, but usually range from $150 to $200.

Any person claiming to act as an Executor must submit a copy of the Will to the Court in a timely fashion, asking that the Court "admit," or formally recognize, the Will.

19

Appointing an Administrator

Where the Decedent has died Intestate, the Court must appoint an Administrator. The various state statutes set forth the priority of those persons who may be appointed to this position. A surviving spouse usually has first claim to serve as the Administrator, unless there is a premarital agreement addressing the issue, or the spouse has previously waived his or her right to serve.

Where there is a Will, the Testator may designate any qualified person or institution (such as a Trust Company) to serve as Executor. (See Question 10 for advice on choosing an Executor.)

If there is no surviving spouse, or if the surviving spouse is not eligible or declines to serve, state statutes will usually provide that Decedent's adult children be appointed. This can result in multiple Co-Administrators. The typical sibling rivalries expected in such a situation can worsen where the Decedent has had children by more than one person and half-siblings become Co-Administrators.

> *A surviving spouse usually has first claim to serve as the Administrator, unless there is a premarital agreement providing otherwise.*

Posting a Bond

The Court will require the Administrator(s) to use funds from the Estate to post a bond with a commercial bonding company. The bond's purpose is to insure the Administrator's faithful accounting for, and administration of, the Estate. If the Administrator violates this duty, the bonding company must compensate the Estate and can then seek reimbursement from the Administrator.

The cost of the bond depends on the value of the assets to be administered. Similar to a life insurance policy, the bond usually has to be paid for through an annual premium. A typical premium for an Estate with assets of $250,000 would be $1,200; for an estate with assets of $500,000, the annual premium should be approximately $1,785.

20

Court Supervision

The Administrator's work will be monitored by the Probate Court. Consequently, the Administrator must obtain Probate Court approval to sell assets, to continue a business, to disburse funds, and so on. Usually, each request for a Court Order requires that a petition be prepared by an attorney and submitted to the Court. These steps obviously result in additional legal fees and Court costs.

Appointing an Executor

Where the Decedent has died Testate, the Will should have designated an Executor and provided for a successor if the original Executor named in the Will cannot or will not serve.

By naming an Executor in his or her Will, the Decedent can avoid competition among family members for appointment as the Administrator. Also, most states allow for "Independent Administration." This means that the Will can authorize the Executor to administer the Estate (sell assets, pay claims, and so on) without Court supervision. Further, the Will can specifically provide that the Executor need not post a bond, which avoids the annual bond premium. Independent Administration also saves expenses because it will be unnecessary to prepare Petitions to the Court requesting approval for certain financial transactions. In sum, a Will can substantially ease the mechanics of the probate proceedings and save time and money, if the Decedent has chosen his or her Executor wisely. ·

Deadlines and Challenges

State statutes require the Will be filed with the Probate Court within a certain period after the Decedent's death. Twelve months is frequently the maximum period. Any challenge to the Will must be filed within a limited period after the Will is admitted to Probate. This period varies from state to state, but rarely extends beyond 12 months.

Public Notice, Public Scrutiny

Probate proceedings almost invariably require that notices of the commencement of the proceedings be published in a newspaper of general circulation. In addition, notices are given by mail to those persons named in the Will, or who are known to be the heirs of the Decedent by operation of law.

> *A Will can substantially ease the mechanics of the Probate proceedings and save time and money, if the Decedent has chosen his or her Executor wisely.*

The Probate process subjects the Decedent's possessions and dealings to public scrutiny. Tongues will wag. For the modest (or those with something to hide), information on the best ways to avoid Probate (Question 3) may prove useful.

Treatment of Creditors

Publication provides notice to the Decedent's creditors to file claims for payment with the Probate Court, usually within six to nine months from the date notice is published. Creditors must check the dates carefully, because claims not filed within a set period after such notice are barred.

The Executor can recognize claims as legitimate or can challenge them. The Court will hold a hearing on challenged claims, with the would-be creditor having the burden of proving the amount owed.

Homestead and Surviving Spouse Allowances

Payments to the Decedent's creditors generally have priority over the distribution of assets to his or her heirs. However, certain exceptions apply with respect to surviving spouses and minor children. Here, most states have provisions referred to as a Homestead Allowance and a Surviving Spouse Support Allowance.

Laws establishing a Homestead Allowance permit a surviving spouse to claim certain assets of the Estate (for example, furniture, family Bible, tools) ahead of creditors. The Court can also award, notwithstanding the claims of creditors, cash to the surviving spouse and minor children as a Homestead Allowance, up to a maximum established by law. These amounts are not substantial—usually around $15,000. However, a few states, particularly Florida and Texas, have unlimited Homestead Allowances.

In addition, many states provide that a surviving spouse be awarded an amount of money sufficient to support her or him (and any minor children) for 12 months after the Decedent's death. The Surviving Spouse Allowance is usually obtained by the filing of a Petition with the Probate Court whereby the surviving spouse sets forth the amount necessary to support him or her (and any minor children) for 12 months in the standard of living they enjoyed at the time of the Decedent's death. Creditors and heirs can object if they believe the request is excessive. After hearing the evidence, the Court will have final say as to the amount of the allowance.

Distributions to Heirs and Length of the Probate Process

Once Allowances have been paid and creditors satisfied, the Administrator or Executor may begin distributing property to the heirs. Where some creditors' claims are in dispute, distribution may begin if enough assets are held back to satisfy the disputed claims should they be proved legitimate. In most cases, some distribution of non-Allowance property will begin within six to 12 months after Probate starts.

Unless the assets of the Decedent subject to Probate proceedings are less than the Homestead and Surviving Spouse Allowances, Probate proceedings hardly ever take less than 12 months.

If there are contested claims, challenges to a request for a Surviving Spouse Allowance, or questions regarding the Estate's ownership of assets, Probate proceedings can easily drag on far longer than 12 months.

Finally, where a Federal Estate Tax Return must be filed (see Chapter 12), the Administrator/Executor may want to keep the Estate in existence until the Tax Return is accepted, or any issues are resolved. This can take several years.

> *Unless the assets of the Decedent subject to Probate proceedings are less than the Homestead and Surviving Spouse Allowances, Probate proceedings hardly ever take less than 12 months.*

Question 3

What Are the Best Ways to Avoid Probate?

An ounce of prevention is worth a pound of cure.
—Benjamin Franklin

The purposes of Probate are:

➲ to pay statutory allowances to a surviving spouse

➲ to satisfy the Decedent's creditors

➲ to transfer the Estate's remaining assets to the Decedent's heirs.

As discussed in Question 2, even in the best of circumstances, Probate involves a certain amount of delay, cost, and public scrutiny. Certain techniques, however, permit an individual to transfer property in such a way that Probate is avoided. These techniques include: transferring ownership to a Trust during one's lifetime (Living Trust); registering title in joint names with rights of survivorship; holding title (for certain assets such as real estate, automobiles, bank accounts, and certificates of deposit) in the owner's name with a "pay on death" provision designating a specific beneficiary inserted in the title; and giving property away during one's lifetime.

Transfers in Trust During Lifetime

Although the authors have been using the lifetime, or *inter vivos*, trust arrangement to enable their clients to avoid Probate for the last 50 years, this device has only become popular recently.

What Does It Mean to "Own" Something?

The starting point for understanding Trusts is to understand what it means to "own" something. When the law says we "own" a piece of property, it means that we possess a certain bundle of rights with regard to that property. These rights include the right to possess the property, to manage it, to use and enjoy it, and to dispose of it.

The law permits an owner to break up this bundle of rights and to distribute various rights to different people. Suppose, for example, that a teenage girl tells her father that her boyfriend is taking her to the mall for a movie and pizza dinner. The father then hands her $10 and tells her to take her younger brother as well. In this case, the father owns property (the $10). He gives the teenager possession and management over the property. But, the teenager may only use the property for the benefit of the younger brother and in the manner directed by the father. She may not spend the money on herself or on her boyfriend. She also may not use it to buy her brother comic books instead of a movie ticket or a hamburger instead of pizza. If the father has not been specific about which movie the brother is to see (parents be warned), the teenager is free to choose it herself or to let her brother decide.

This arrangement is basically what happens with a Trust. Most Trusts are established by a document in which a person with property (the Grantor) transfers the rights to hold and manage the property to a person or persons (the Trustee or Trustees) for the benefit of another person or persons (the Beneficiary or Beneficiaries). A Trustee is considered to have "nominal," or "legal,"ownership of this property, while the Beneficiary/Beneficiaries has/have "beneficial" ownership. In our example, the father is the Grantor; the teenage daughter is the Trustee, and the younger brother is the Beneficiary.

Basic Elements of a Trust Agreement

A Trust Agreement should set forth, in detail, the terms and conditions relating to the Trustee's and Beneficiaries' rights and duties. The Trust Agreement should also provide instructions on how the Trustee should distribute and use the property initially placed in the Trust, as well as the income arising from the property, such as interest, dividends, rents and the like.

> *The starting point for understanding Trusts is to understand what it means to "own" something.*

To maintain flexibility for the Grantor, the Trust Agreement should provide that the Grantor may, in his or her sole judgment, alter, amend, or revoke the Trust Agreement, or to withdraw assets from the Trust, at any time during his or her lifetime.

It is also possible for a Grantor to name him- or herself as both the Trustee and Beneficiary during his or her lifetime. Thus, an individual can:

- ➲ transfer hisos her assets to the Trust, which is a separate legal entity.
- ➲ continue to manage those assets as the Trustee.
- ➲ continue to receive the income for his or her life as the Beneficiary.

This arrangement is frequently referred to as a Grantor Trust."

When the Grantor Dies

Upon the Grantor's death, the Trust as a separate legal entity continues in existence. The Trust Agreement should provide for a successor Trustee/Trustees as well as secondary Beneficiary/Beneficiaries. Upon the Grantor's death, and except in limited situations, the Trust can no longer be amended or revoked;

it becomes "irrevocable." This said, many states now permit the Beneficiaries of a trust to seek a judge's permission to amend or revoke a Trust if such changes would be in the best interests of all parties and the rights of all Beneficiaries are protected. Also, the Trust Agreement can give to a person referred to as a "Trust Protector" the right to amend the trust in his sole judgment if the law changes in such a way that the Beneficiaries' interests would otherwise be hurt.

In giving the property to the Trust during his lifetime, the Grantor has ceased to "own" the property. As a result, when the Grantor dies, the property in the Trust is *not* subject to Probate. The terms of the Trust Agreement should instruct the Trustee how to distribute the property in the Trust (both the initial property and the income it has generated) to the Beneficiaries, who may be the Grantor's spouse, children, or other persons (including charities).

Limits on What a Trust Can Do

In essence, the Trust serves as a Will without the necessity of Probate. But a Grantor may not transfer property to a Trust in order to hinder his creditors. In such cases, the creditors may have a court unwind the transfer so they can use the property to satisfy the debts owed them.

Although a Living Trust can, to a great degree, function as a Will, a Grantor should still have a Will to cover certain adminis-trative matters (filing final income-tax returns, disposing of per-sonal items). Also, the Will should typically provide that any property that has not been transferred to the Trust prior to death be con-tributed to the Trust ("poured over" to the Trust) to be managed and distributed in the same manner as the other Trust assets.

Joint Tenancy/Ownership With Rights of Survivorship (JTWROS)

This entire subject will be covered in detail in Question 4; however, for this purpose (to avoid Probate), we should mention that it is possible to have the ownership of property held in the names of two persons—whether or not they are married—and to provide that, upon the death of the first to die, the survivor becomes the sole owner of that property. If property is held in JTWROS, each party has ownership rights while both are alive.

As a result of JTWROS, full ownership automatically passes by operation of law to the survivor without the necessity of any Will or Probate proceedings. The vast majority of homes owned by married couples are owned as JTWROS, as are many bank accounts, brokerage accounts, and other investment assets.

Transfer-on-Death Provisions

Most states permit the owner of property to add language to the title of certain assets providing that, upon the death of the owner, title to such assets automatically passes to another person. This arrangement differs from joint property with rights of survivorship in that the designated recipient has absolutely no rights in and to the property while the owner is alive. Also, if the designated recipient dies before the owner, the title will be unaffected. Further, the owner may change the designated recipient by either eliminating the provision or naming another person. This can be done unilaterally and without informing the originally designated recipient.

> *As a result of JOWROS, full ownership automatically passes by operation of law to the survivor without the necessity of any Will or Probate proceedings.*

This type of ownership registration is particularly useful with respect to cars, boats and modest bank accounts, or certificates of deposit. Some states now permit real estate to be transferred by means of deeds, which are recorded prior to the owner's death, but which provide that, upon death, title transfers to the designated recipient. Again, prior to death, the owner can record a new deed and cancel or change the designated post-death recipient. One obvious downside to this registration is that if the designated recipient dies before the owner, the property becomes subject to Probate proceedings upon the owner's death unless the owner has changed the "pay on death" to a new recipient.

Gifts During Lifetime

Obviously, those assets gifted by the decedent during his or her lifetime and which are no longer owned at death will not be subject to Probate. However, as a practical matter, and except for jewelry and other items of personal property, we have not seen many persons make substantial gifts during their lifetimes other than in connection with their estate tax planning. These concepts will be discussed in detail in Questions 9 and 13.

Question 4

when Can joint Property Be a Trap for the Unwary?

...with all my worldly goods I thee endow...
—traditional wedding vows

When most people speak of joint property, they are probably thinking of property owned jointly by a husband and a wife with the understanding that, upon the death of either spouse, the survivor will become the sole owner of the property. However, there are several forms of joint ownership of property.

Tenancies by the Entireties

If a husband and wife acquire property in both their names, that ownership is referred to in several states as "Tenancies by the Entireties." This basically means that both spouses must consent to any sale or transfer of the property to a third party and that, upon the death of the first to die, the survivor will automatically and immediately become the sole owner.

A Tenancy by the Entireties offers unique protection against creditors. With one exception, a creditor of only one spouse may not sever the spouses' joint ownership. As a result, the creditor cannot attach the half of the property that belongs to the debtor spouse. The exception applies to tax debts owed by a spouse to the federal government. And, of course, if both spouses owe the creditor, the creditor can attach the entire property.

Traditionally, only husbands and wives have been allowed to own property as Tenants by the Entireties, but "civil unions" and "gay marriages," as they may exist from state to state, may broaden the types of couples entitled to this form of ownership.

Joint Tenancy/Ownership With Rights of Survivorship (JTWROS)

Spouses may also own property as JTWROS. In this case, upon the death of either spouse, the survivor automatically and immediately becomes the sole owner. However, where one spouse incurs debts to a creditor, that creditor can, through a court proceeding, usually sever joint ownership of the property and then use the debtor's half to satisfy the amount owed.

> *Where one spouse incurs debts to a creditor, that creditor can usually sever joint ownership of the property and then use the debtor's half to satisfy the amount owed.*

Joint Tenants with Rights of Survivorship is winner take all. The joint tenants need not be spouses or civil-union partners. Upon the death of one of the joint tenants, the survivor immediately becomes the owner of the entire property. It is possible for Joint Tenants with Rights of Survivorship to own the property other than on a 50/50 basis. For example, a deed to a farm can state, "John Smith, as to an undivided 75 percent interest, and Joe Brown as to an undivided 25 percent interest, as Joint Tenants with rights of survivorship." Although it is not common, it is legally possible to have more than two JTWROS. In such a situation, the last surviving tenant will become the ultimate sole owner. Unless the title document to the property specifically states what each tenant's respective percentage interest is (whether JTWROS or Tenants-in-Common), they are deemed to own it equally. Thus, if there are two joint tenants, each has a 1/2 interest; if three joint tenants, each has a 1/3 interest.

Tenants-in-Common

Another form of joint ownership is known as "Tenancies-in-Common." This form of ownership does not provide for the survivor to acquire the interest of a deceased co-owner. Each Tenant-in-Common (there may be two or more) has the right to transfer his or her interest during lifetime and to leave that interest to his or her heirs at death. Again, unless specific percentages of the Tenants'-in-Common interests are set forth, they will be presumed to own the property in equal shares. Because there is no survivorship attribute, the interest of a Tenant-in-Common will not avoid probate at the death of any joint owner.

A frequent occasion where Tenancy-in-Common arises is when a parent dies with or without a Will and leaves assets which are not easily divisible (for example, a farm or a residence). Where there is no Will (and no surviving spouse), state law will deem the children to inherit as Tenants-in-Common. If there is a Will that does no more than leave a piece of property to children equally, under the law of most States, the children will inherit that property as Tenants-in-Common.

A positive aspect of a Tenancy-in-Common may be that each Tenant can control his or her interest. The downside is that any Tenant-in-Common can file a lawsuit to partition and sell the property. Except in rare cases, a partition suit usually results in the parties receiving less than a true fair market value of the property, because would-be buyers know the property must be sold.

Although ownership of property as Tenants by the Entireties, or as Joint Tenants with Rights of Survivorship, permits the passage of ownership without the necessity of Probate proceedings, such ownership arrangements also prohibit any restrictions on the survivor. Property which is owned as JTWROS, or as Tenants by the Entireties, passes outside the Will and is therefore unaffected by its provisions.

There is a presumption in most states that if property is owned by a husband and wife without a specific designation as to the type of joint ownership, it is deemed to be either Tenants by the Entireties or JTWROS depending on the state. Conversely, if property is owned jointly by persons who are not married to each other, they are deemed to be Tenants-in-Common *unless* the title specifically states they are to be JTWROS.

The Probate-avoiding features of JTWROS and Tenancies by the Entireties have led to their being called a "poor man's Will." But, the lack of restrictions on the survivor means that these forms of ownership can lead to unexpected and unfortunate consequences.

> *There is a presumption in most states that if property is owned by a husband and wife without specific designation as to the type of joint ownership, it is deemed to be either Tenants by Entireties or JTWROS depending on the state.*

A real-life example of the problems that can arise involves a widow who had three grown children. Two lived out of town, one lived nearby. The child who lived nearby drove her mother to the supermarket, arranged her mother's visits to the doctor, and managed her mother's finances. For convenience, the mother's bank account and certificates of deposit had been placed in joint names with this child so the child could arrange for payment of the mother's bills, depositing of her mother's social-security checks and stock dividends, and dealing with the mother's bank and credit-card company, and so on. The mother had a Will that provided for all of her assets to be divided equally among her three children. However, upon the mother's death, the money in the joint bank account and joint certificates of deposit transferred automatically and entirely to this one child, who decided that she was entitled to these assets in light of the care she alone had given the mother. Aside from whatever unfairness this decision might have created, it also led to a permanent rift in the family.

There was, of course, a very simple way to enable the child to handle her mother's affairs while avoiding the situation previously described: the parent could and should have had a document prepared and signed by the caretaker child acknowledging that the joint ownership was for convenience only and agreeing to divide the funds equally with her siblings upon the mother's death. Copies of this document should have been given to all of the children, with a copy attached to the Will.

Another real-life situation where joint property ownership proved disastrous was the following: a man was killed in an auto accident, leaving behind a wife and two young children. The widow received substantial life-insurance proceeds as well as a settlement from the accident. She, then, had a Will prepared providing that upon her death, her assets would go to her two children; if they were still minors at the time of her death, her sister would act at their Trustee.

Subsequently, the widow married a fine gentleman who owned his own business. After a couple of years of marriage, she and her second husband decided to purchase a larger retail business. The woman invested the funds she had received from her first husband's death, and the man sold his existing business and invested the proceeds. They took title to the new business as Tenants by the Entireties.

The business was a success. But, unfortunately, only about three years later the woman died suddenly of an aneurysm. The sister, seeking to protect the interests of the two children from the first marriage, demanded that half of the business be transferred to her as Trustee for the two children. Litigation ensued, and the court found that because the husband and wife had owned the business as Tenants by the Entirety, upon the wife's death the second husband had become the sole owner. The children received absolutely nothing.

Final Thoughts

All too often, married couples believe they should own all property jointly with Rights of Survivorship. The foregoing actual cases show how joint property can be a trap for the unwary. In most situations, there is probably nothing wrong with having the family residence, as well as a bank account for everyday expenses, owned in joint names. However, when the parties acquire investment assets, or are parties to second marriages, much thought should be given before owning assets in this manner.

Question 5

When Should I Write My Own Will?

It has been said that a lawyer who represents himself has a fool for a client. The authors believe that a layman who represents himself has an even bigger fool for a client.

Holographic Wills

A Will written by the Testator himself is called a "Holographic Will." The word "Holographic" is a combination of two Greek words meaning "whole" and "written." Originally, the law required that a Holographic Will be: entirely handwritten by the Testator, and signed by him or her. However, there have been cases where a hand-printed Will was accepted as a Holographic Will.

The requirement that the document be in the Testator's own handwriting is intended to guard against forgery because Holographic Wills do not require witnesses to attest to the Testator's signature.

The Uniform Probate Code ("UPC") is a body of model rules drafted by several expert legal scholars which authorizes Holographic Wills, §2-502(b). The legislatures of nearly 20 States have enacted the UPC, although some have done so with modifications. In addition, some States which have not adopted the UPC also recognize Holographic Wills (for example, California and Tennessee).

The UPC states that a Will is valid as a Holographic Will, whether or not witnessed, if the signature and material portions of the document are in the Testator's handwriting. However, some States require that the document be entirely handwritten; others require that the document be dated because without a date, it may be impossible to determine whether the undated Holographic Will is the "Last Will" of the Testator.

> *Some states require that Holographic Wills be entirely handwritten.*

Holographic Wills have generated much litigation, which has generally involved three areas:

1. the requirement in many States that the Holographic Will be dated
2. the requirement in several States that such Wills be *entirely* in the Decedent's handwriting
3. a determination of the Decedent's intent

Because many persons who wrote their own Wills frequently failed to express themselves clearly, their Holographic Wills resulted in litigation.

In a more humorous vein, we should note actual situations where Holographic Wills which were written on a petticoat, or scratched on a tractor fender, or written on a woman's purse have been accepted by courts as Holographic Wills.

Pre-Printed Wills

In addition to the Testator actually writing his or her own Will, the use of pre-printed, fill-in-the-blank forms has generated a new set of problems.

It is now possible to acquire printed Will forms in stationery and office supply stores, as well as over the Internet. These forms have pre-printed language, with the Testator expected to fill in certain blanks. In those States requiring that a Holographic Will be entirely in the Testator's handwriting, such pre-printed forms may *fail* to constitute a Holographic Will. In other States requiring that only "material" provisions (as opposed to all provisions) be in the Testator's handwriting, such a form document may be a valid Will even though immaterial parts, such as the date or introductory wording, were pre-printed or stamped. A valid Holographic Will might even be executed on some printed Will forms if the printed portion were eliminated and the handwritten portion sufficiently evidenced the Testator's intent.

The law books are, unfortunately, filled with cases arising from Holographic Wills, or "do-it-yourself" printed form Wills. Because there is a public demand for a legally, valid do-it-yourself Will that can be written on a printed form, several States have now authorized simple statutory "fill-in-the-form" Wills. The form usually provides spaces for the Testator to name the beneficiaries or the specific property to be given to certain persons. California and Michigan are two States permitting the fill-in-the-blanks form Wills.

However, some States which permit the do-it-yourself form Wills still require that they be signed and witnessed and/or notarized to the same degree as all other Wills. When the Will is required to be signed by the Testator, and dated and signed by witnesses, it is no longer a true Holographic Will. Notwithstanding the fact that certain States have tried to make the procedure available to their citizens, a number of fill-in-the-blank Wills have been rejected by the Probate Courts because they were improperly completed or executed. We cannot over-emphasize the importance of having all Wills comply with the statutory requirements of the particular State with respect to the execution of the Will, the dating, the witnessing and, in several States, the acknowledgment by a person authorized to administer oaths, such as a notary public.

Handwritten Changes to a Will

Another situation where the validity of a Holographic Will comes into question is when a Testator has a valid Will but then, in his or her own handwriting, adds new or different provisions ("interlineates the Will"). These situations have led to much litigation if the State acknowledges Holographic Wills; to the extent that material portions are in the Testator's handwriting, the handwritten interlineations or amendments may be accepted. However, if the court determines that the handwritten interlineations do not constitute material portions of the Will, the entire document may be rejected for Probate. If State law requires that the entire document be in the handwriting of the Testator, the handwritten amendments or interlineations will probably not be recognized, whether substantial or not.

If a person is going to use a pre-printed form and fill-in-the-blanks, it is critical that he or she make absolutely certain that the applicable State law does not require that the Will be wholly in the Testator's handwriting. There are some cases where the courts ignored the preprinted language to determine whether the handwritten language by itself constituted a valid Will. This type of issue should never arise. We recommend that a layman not seek to write his or her own Will, use a fill-in-the-blanks form, or try to make his or her own changes by hand.

> *If the court determines that handwritten interlineations do not constitute material portions of a Holographic Will, the entire document may be rejected for Probate.*

However, if one insists on using a pre-printed, fill-in-the-blanks form, or acts as an original draftsman, we strongly suggest that the document be dated (month, day, and year), signed by the Testator in the presence of at least two adult persons who have no financial interest in the Will and who, then, sign as witnesses. The Will should also be notarized, which is a service that a bank branch will usually provide for free or for a nominal charge (often less than $10). Thus, the Testator has avoided the lawyer's office, and should have a valid Will. By following the procedures for dating and having the witnesses sign the Will, it should not be deemed a Holographic Will.

Penny Wise and Pound Foolish

Remember that the validity of the Will, or the clarity of its provisions, will not be tested until after the Decedent's death. At that point, it is too late to cure any defect. It is impossible to visit Memorial Park Cemetery to have a codicil signed, or to ask the Decedent what was his or her intent with respect to a Holographic Will.

No one likes paying legal fees, but hiring a reputable, experienced attorney who can do the work correctly and efficiently will be money well spent. The fact that pre-printed forms come with disclaimers nearly as long as (and often better drafted than) the forms themselves should tell you something.

Trying to write your own Will or to use a pre-printed form is penny wise and pound foolish. Don't do it.

Question 6

How Much/Little Can I Leave My Spouse?

> *If I were your wife,*
> *I would put poison in your coffee.*
> —Nancy Astor (to Winston Churchill)

> *And if I were your husband, I would drink it.*
> —Winston Churchill (in reply)

Like many things in life, the question posed by this chapter is not all black or white. There will be situations where a Decedent leaves less than he or she could to a beloved spouse. There will also be cases where a Decedent arranges to leave as little as possible to his or her spouse and can justifiably grumble that it is too much.

How Much Can I Leave?

You can leave all of your Estate to a surviving spouse. The law does not require that anything be left to children or other relatives, not even the proverbial dollar.

As discussed in Question 4, our preferred route for transferring sizeable assets to a surviving spouse is through a Trust. Suffice it to say here that a Trust generally:

41

- ⮞ avoids probate
- ⮞ helps protect assets from waste or diversion
- ⮞ provides maximum flexibility for Estate Tax planning

For these reasons, a loving spouse may sometimes bequeath the bulk of his or her Estate to a Trust rather than directly to his or her surviving spouse.

How Little Can I Leave?

This question arises more frequently than one might expect. The answer depends upon the law of the state in which the couple reside.

The Elective Share

In general, no state permits you to leave nothing to a surviving spouse, no matter how unloving, uncaring, or unfaithful that spouse has been. In this regard, the various states have carried over a centuries-old English tradition entitling a widow to choose between: (1) the share left her under her late husband's Will; and (2) the minimum share provided for by statute. This minimum statutory amount is called the "elective share." In recent times, in the United States, the right to an elective share has also been extended to widowers.

Many, but not all, states set the elective share at the amount the surviving spouse would have received had the deceased Grantor spouse died without a Will (see Question 1). Note that this amount even includes assets which are not "marital property" and to which the surviving spouse would have had no claim had there been a divorce.

The states differ, however, on how to calculate the elective share. Several states provide that the elective share only includes those assets subject to Probate (the Probate Estate).

This limitation would appear to permit a spouse to reduce the elective share prior to death by:

1. making gifts to third persons (including placing property in joint name with these persons)

or

2. transferring assets to a Trust

But getting around the law's basic protection of widows/widowers is not so simple. In calculating the elective share, some states permit the surviving spouse to include assets the deceased spouse gave away during his or her lifetime, if such gifts were made in "fraud of the spouse's rights." Gifts are most likely to be considered fraudulent if they took place shortly before death and/or without the surviving spouse's knowledge. Conversely, gifts will stand a better chance of surviving court scrutiny if the surviving spouse knew of the gifts and failed to object.

> *Gifts are most likely to be considered fradulent if they took place shortly befor death and/or without the surviving spouse's knowledge.*

Trusts raise a more complex set of questions. Some states include assets contributed to a Revocable Living Trust (See Question 4) in the elective-share calculation, on the grounds that the spouse retained ultimate control over the assets until death. For the same reason, it will be harder—but not necessarily impossible—to include assets contributed to an Irrevocable Trust; in such cases, the spouse has parted with control prior to death. Finally, where the Trust, revocable or irrevocable, has made some provision for the surviving spouse, it may be harder for that spouse to have the Trust assets included in the elective share.

To summarize the factors a court may consider in fixing the elective-share amount:

More likely to be included in elective share:	Less likely to be included in elective share:

➡ Gifts made immediately before Death
➡ Gifts made without spouse's knowledge or consent
	➡ Gifts made long before Death
	➡ Gifts made:
	  ➡ with spouse's consent
	    or
	  ➡ where spouse has known about gift and failed to object

➡ Transfers to Revocable Trust ➡ Transfers to Irrevocable Trust with no provision for surviving spouse	➡ Transfers to Irrevocable Trust ➡ Transfers to Irrevocable Trust that provides for surviving spouse

Adjustments to the Elective-Share Amount

Some states reduce the elective share by any asset the surviving spouse may have acquired as a surviving joint tenant.

Control

Choosing the elective share provides the surviving spouse with not only a minimum percentage of the Probate Estate, but also with outright control of this percentage.

It often happens that a spouse leaves substantial money for his or her widow/widower in Trust. The Trust provides that the income is payable to the surviving spouse for life, with the assets to be distributed to designated beneficiaries upon the surviving spouse's death. Typically, the Trustee is someone other than the surviving spouse.

Although the surviving spouse may receive income from the Trust for his/her lifetime, he or she has no control over the assets.

Moreover, the surviving spouse may not want to see all of the assets ultimately go to the designated beneficiaries, particularly if they are not his or her children.

In this situation, the Decedent's spouse has the right to reject the Trust and to "take against the Will." In this event, he or she will receive the elective-share amount, which might be only a third, or less, of the total assets in the Trust. But, the surviving spouse will own this amount outright.

Making the Election

The surviving spouse has a limited period of time to choose between the elective share and the amount left him/her by the Will or other Trust. This period varies from state to state, but is usually somewhere between six and nine months. Because the rules governing the calculation can be complex, and vary from state to state, the surviving spouse should consult an attorney before making a decision, particularly if the Decedent:

- ➲ left property in different states
- ➲ tried to reduce the elective share through gifts or other means

If the surviving spouse is legally incompetent, a conservator, guardian, or attorney-in-fact may make the election on his/her behalf.

Other Considerations

Effect of Premarital Agreement

Although Premarital Agreements will be discussed, in detail, in Question 15, the existence of such an Agreement is relevant to this chapter. Prior to their marriage, a couple can enter into a Premarital Agreement which addresses the issues relating to the rights of each spouse to share in the assets of the other in the event of a divorce or death. The Agreement can provide for a complete waiver of all elective and other statutory rights, or can provide for a fixed dollar amount, or a fixed percentage of the value of

45

the deceased spouse's assets. It is not uncommon to have the fixed amount or percentage tied to the length of the marriage. Thus, the longer the parties were married, the greater the benefit to the surviving spouse. Also, if one party has considerably more assets than the other when the Premarital Agreement is negotiated, we frequently find that the "wealthy" party will waive all rights to participate in the other's Estate, but the "poorer" party will be given certain benefits in the Estate of the wealthy spouse.

> *Under some premarital agreements, the longer the parties were married, the greater the benefit to the surviving spouse.*

The elective-share decision can also affect eligibility for welfare, Medicaid, and other government programs for the poor. Courts have recently considered situations where a widow/widower has been left virtually no assets in his or her own name but has the right to a sizeable elective share. (Often the Decedent, aided by a cunning lawyer, has left assets in a Trust or bequeathed them to the couple's children, so that the surviving spouse will qualify as "poor" for the sake of government programs, even though the Trust, or children, can more than satisfy the surviving spouse's needs.) Some recent cases have held that in these situations, the surviving spouse must either take the elective share from the Decedent's estate—and thereby gain assets to be used for her support—or become ineligible for state benefits.

Question 7

When Is It Fair to Treat My Children Unequally?

Now Israel loved Joseph more than all his children, because he [was] the son of his old age: and he made him a coat of [many] colours. And when his brethren saw that their father loved him more than all his brethren, they hated him, and could not speak peaceably unto him.

—Genesis 37:3-4

Why Equal Is Easy, But Not Always Equitable

Anyone who doesn't believe human beings have an innate sense of justice has never tried to dishout ice cream among several children.

From the Bible to Shakespeare to the Jerry Springer Show, nothing arouses passions, jealousies, and outright hatreds more than feelings of injustice within a family. And nothing stands a greater chance of creating or unleashing such feelings than a Will. The Will is a parent's or grandparent's last word. To many, it represents the last act of parental love and acceptance, or of disappointment and rejection. For sibling rivals, the division of an inheritance serves as the final round, the one played for "all the marbles," with whatever moderating influence the parent/grandparent might have exercised gone for good.

Writing a Will can therefore be daunting. You not only have to face your own death but potential emotional and financial upset within your family. In such circumstances, most people opt for equal shares for all their children. As we have seen in Question 1 (What Happens if I Die Without a Will?), equal shares for every child is the law's background rule. Over your lifetime, equal shares for everybody has probably been the rule you applied to any number of activities, including dishing out ice cream. Equal shares for everybody seems natural and straightforward. It is easy.

But equal is not always equitable. As we discuss in the sections that follow, there are many circumstances where an equal distribution of property among children may be unfair, where such a distribution can create real and unnecessary hardships for some or all of your descendants, and where it can foster or inflame resentments that will last more than one lifetime.

This chapter will give no pat answers about how to divide your property. Life is too complicated, and family situations, too varied. But the chapter will flag the most important situations you will have to think through if you want to do right by your loved ones—if you want them to live in peace while you rest in peace.

Why Your Will Must Name All of Your Children

There is a common misperception that a Will must leave each child at least $1. This misperception exists because the law treats failure to mention a child as an oversight. The law then permits that child to claim the same share of property which he or she would have been entitled to if the parent had died without a Will. To avoid this situation, people often leave each child at least $1 to ensure mentioning them.

The better course of action is to identify your spouse and each of your children by name at the beginning of your Will. If, at the time that you draw up or revise your Will, additional children are yet be born, your Will should also indicate how they are to be treated. Also mention any grandchildren who have been born and give consideration to grandchildren yet to be born. In addition, you should give thought to distinctions between or among natural (grand)children, adopted (grand)children, step-(grand)children, and the like.

In years past, the law's background rule disinherited a man's illegitimate children. Such a blanket rule is now unconstitutional. As a consequence, your Will should and must name any illegitimate children of whom you are aware, even if only to deny them any bequests. If any wild oats you have sewn might have sprouted, your Will should also indicate how they should be treated, even if you cannot name them individually. The same advice applies to illegitimate grandchildren or other descendants.

One background rule that does remain in effect presumes that the children of a married woman have been fathered by her husband. Modern DNA testing can remove any doubts as to paternity. The Will can require proof, where such doubts exist, but testing should not be put off until after you die.

Disclosing infidelity is never pleasant. However, because an illegitimate child (if left unmentioned) can take against the Will, it is better for the surprise to happen when the Will is read (if not earlier) than when the illegitimate child lays claim to his share in the Probate court.

> *Your Will should and must name any illegitimate children of whom you are aware.*

Real-Life Examples of Unequal Being Fair

When Your Children Are at Different Ages and Stages in Life

It costs almost $175,000 to raise a child to the age of 18. A four-year college education can run anywhere from $20,000 to $200,000. Where you have paid for the upbringing and education of older children, it is fair to leave more money to the younger ones. Similarly, if you have helped out some children, but not others, through gifts or loans, you might want to take these differences into account when dividing your property.

When You Have a Special-Needs Child

A mentally or physically disabled child will likely require more than his or her able-bodied siblings. But be careful: leaving property to a disabled child can disqualify that child for various kinds of governmental assistance, or can entitle the government to take some or all of the money you have bequeathed.

You can avoid these risks by establishing a "special needs trust." We discuss the general concept and use of trusts in Question 8. Bear in mind, though, that the special-needs area and governmental-assistance rules are highly technical and often inflexible. Seek expert advice. (See Question 20: How Do I Find and Work with a Lawyer or Accountant?)

When the Family Tree Is Lop-Sided

By choice or fortune, some people have more children than others. When these people are your children, figuring out the right thing to do can be a challenge.

When Is It Fair To Treat My Children Unequally?

As the following figure shows, giving money equally to your children can leave your grandchildren with widely varying amounts of wealth:

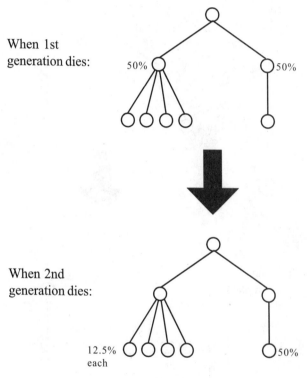

Per Stirpes
(Wealth flows evenly along the family tree)

When 1st generation dies:

When 2nd generation dies:

One alternative combines equal gifts to children with equal gifts to grandchildren. This combination treats the two branches unequally but might be more fair:

Combination of Per Stirpes and Per Capita

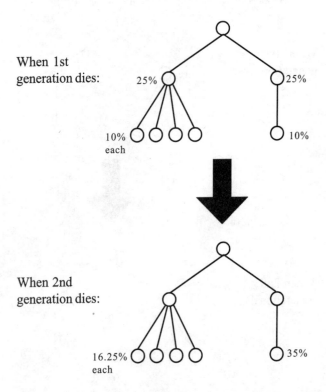

When 1st generation dies:

25%   25%

10% each   10%

When 2nd generation dies:

16.25% each   35%

Of course, real-world cases with many children, multiple spouses, half-children, step children, and so on, can rapidly grow complex. Your goal should be rough justice, within the limits of what can be foreseen and implemented.

When a Child (or Child-in-Law) Has Been a Devoted Caregiver

The duty for caring for an aging parent often falls unevenly on the children. This is sometimes due to geographic proximity, sometimes to different levels of availability or personal responsibility. Often, the burden falls on a daughter-in-law.

Fairness may require you to recognize uneven burdens with uneven bequests.

When There Is a Prodigal Son/Daughter

There may be cases where a child has merited disapproval to the point where you wish to leave them less than you are leaving his or her siblings, or even leave him or her nothing. (There are also cases where parents have chosen to leave the prodigal child more than the responsible children because he or she needs more.)

A less clear-cut case arises where children are equally deserving but have unequal needs. For example, one child might have become an investment banker or married into wealth, while another has become a schoolteacher.

With limited exceptions, your Will *should* explain why you have decided to treat children unequally or to leave someone nothing. One exception is where disapproval is particularly strong; here, it is better simply to say, "for reasons well known to him or her." Another exception is where the disapproval arises from a reason a court might have trouble enforcing on public-policy grounds. So, for example, it is likely that a court will refuse to enforce a Will provision that disinherits a child "for marrying a person of another race or faith."

How You Can Lessen the Chances of Animosity or a Court Battle

Give Gifts During Your Lifetime

As discussed in Question 2, your Will is a public document. But there is nothing to prevent you from confidentially helping a needy, deserving, or favored child or grandchild while you are still alive.

Disinherit Anyone Who Contests the Will

Your Will can provide for the automatic disinheritance of anyone who contests it. Courts do not like these provisions, but, if properly drafted, they are generally enforceable.

> *Bequests that have nothing to do with the degree of a parent's love or respect can take on deeply hurtful and divisive meanings.*

Don't Equate Money With Love in Your Will or in Your Life

People often treat Wills as final report cards on the people named in them. Bequests that have nothing to do with the degree of a parent's love or respect can take on deeply hurtful and divisive meanings. Remember that your property will be limited, but that your praise, love, and gratitude need not be. Don't leave your affections unsaid in your letters, in your Will, or in your life.

Question 8

How Should I Leave Money or Property to Someone Not Old or Wise Enough to Manage It?

We grow old too soon and wise too late.
—German Proverb

For many families, making money is easier than keeping it. The very young and very old often simply cannot look after themselves. Between these two extremes of age lie situations in which offspring are no longer minors, but lack financial maturity and judgment, or in which loved ones may be legally competent, but cannot properly manage their affairs. You should not overlook the possibility of ceasing to be able to take care of yourself due to physical or mental illness.

Common wisdom holds that no one can manage property better than the person who has earned it. Parents therefore hesitate to leave money, outright, to children who lack either the discipline or the skills needed to manage money well. An irony of life is that adversity and want often drive one generation to labor and sacrifice so the next generation will know financial security. Then, this hard-won security causes the next generation to spurn the labor and sacrifice needed to keep adversity and want from coming back.

Trusts

A Trust Agreement, established during life (Living Trust), or in a Will (Testamentary Trust), is probably the best way to provide for the security of persons unable to manage funds for their own benefit. (See Chapter 3 for an introduction to Trusts.)

A Trust Agreement offers virtually unlimited flexibility. The Trust Agreement can give the Trustee discretion, or instruct him or her, to pay all, some, or none of the income from the Trust to or for the benefit of the Beneficiaries. Also, the Trustee can be authorized to dip into (encroach upon) the principal of the Trust where current income is insufficient or the Beneficiary has an unusual, deserving need (for example, home purchase, new business, and so on) In Question 10, we explore the question of how to select a good Trustee.

Transfers in Installments

A middle ground between giving property outright to an heir and tying it up in trust through the heir's lifetime is to release money in *installments*. This way, if the heir fumbles with the first installment, the entire inheritance has not been lost, and succeeding installments will hopefully be handled with more wisdom and care.

There is no rule or law that regulates either the number of installments or the ages at which installments should be paid. Parents seem to gravitate toward three installments payable at ages 25, 30, and 35, or possibly 30, 35, and 40. Because there are no guidelines as to the "correct" ages, you should rely upon your assessment of your children's developing maturity and abilities. Bear in mind that you don't have to treat all children the same. Responsible children can receive everything outright, while the "wild child," or "black sheep" in the family, might have his or her inheritance held in trust for certain periods of time, or even for his or her entire life.

Rather than fixing the installment periods in the Trust Agreement, some Grantors let the Trustee decide when the principal should be distributed to the Beneficiaries. We have drawn documents which provide that, as and when the Trustee determines that the Beneficiary has established mature judgment and has demonstrated the ability to responsibly manage assets, the Trustee may distribute the principal to that child. This approach will permit great flexibility, as well as the distribution to different children at different ages.

> *We recommend that, as minor children attain certain ages, they become a Co-Trustee for their respective shares of the Trust Estate.*

While installment payments make sense, we also recommend that, as minor children attain certain ages, they become a Co-Trustee for their respective shares of the Trust Estate. This encourages them to learn money management and, hopefully, to establish an amicable working arrangement with the more experienced Trustee.

Custodianship

In the late 1950s, an additional technique was introduced to provide financial security for minors. This technique was promoted through the Uniform Gifts to Minors Act (UGMA), a version of which has been adopted in all of the states. The UGMA permits a Grantor to appoint a Custodian to receive property for the benefit of a minor and to hold and reinvest this property until the minor attains the age of majority.

Some states grant the Custodian powers similar to those of a Trustee; other states greatly restrict the Custodian's rights regarding investments, distributions, and so on. Another point of difference between a Trust and Custodianship is that, while a single Trust may be created to take care of several Beneficiaries, a custodial account is for one person only. Also, UGMAs *require* that the assets held by the Custodian be transferred directly to the Beneficiary when he or she reaches the age of 21, or in some states, age 18. For modest sums of money, hand over of control to an 18- or 21 year-old may not be a problem. However, if the gifts were large, or the assets increased in value between the date of the original gift and the date of required distribution, the Grantor might not wish to see the money transferred to a youth with no experience managing funds, who can be easily manipulated by others.

Common Concerns

Special Needs Trust

In the past, parents of physically disabled or mentally retarded children found themselves in a Catch-22. The parents wanted to set aside money for these children, but establishing Trusts for them disqualified them from certain types of means-tested governmental assistance, such as Social Security Disability Insurance.

In response, a number of states enacted rules for "Special Needs Trusts." A Special Needs Trust is established in the same manner as other Trusts, but should not disqualify a Beneficiary from governmental assistance. Under a Special Needs Trust, the Trust income and principal may **not** be used to provide basic support for the Beneficiary. The funds may only be used for *supplemental* care: medical and dental care, educational expenses, entertainment, vacations, and so on. Distributions from a Special Needs Trust must be made to the provider of the supplemental services, not to the Beneficiary.

Special Needs Trusts are a very technical area. Unless the rules are followed, State laws may permit recovery (recapture) from the Trust, or the child, of an amount equal to the governmental assistance paid. Any Agreement establishing a Special Needs Trust should, therefore, be drafted by a knowledgeable attorney with particular care given to selecting the Trustee.

Common Concerns

Sons- and Daughters-in-Law

Parents often disapprove of their children's choice of spouses. As a result, parents worry that giving an inheritance outright to a child will enable the child-in-law to take and squander the money. Parents additionally worry that should the child divorce, the divorce court will award a large chunk of the inheritance to the disliked child-in-law.

Here again, our trusty Trust Agreement can nip these problems in the bud. The child's share can be placed in Trust for his or her life, with the child receiving the income periodically (usually every three months). The Trustee can have the right to encroach upon the principal for the child's benefit, or for the benefit and education of grandchildren. In this manner, the child has the benefit of the funds, but the child-in-law cannot get to the principal. Parents can rest in peace.

Spendthrift Children

Parents of a spendthrift child fret that the child's creditors will seek to attach the child's inheritance. Placing the assets in Trust and specifically providing that the child may not assign his or her interest in the Trust keeps creditors at bay. This concept is referred to as a *Spendthrift Trust*.

Your Own Decline

Some prudent clients even anticipate their own declining abilities, particularly where there are early signs, or a family history, of senility or debilitating illness. In such cases, clients establish a Living Trust with themselves as Grantor and Beneficiary. The Trust Agreement provides that in the event the Grantor's physician certifies that the Grantor is unable to manage his or her affairs because of a physical or mental condition, the Grantor, if acting as Trustee, will be succeeded by a person identified in the Agreement. This arrangement sidesteps situations where the Grantor is legally "competent" but far past the point of being able to manage his or her affairs properly, to say nothing of situations involving embarrassing and acrimonious competency hearings.

Question 9

How Should I Divide the Indivisible, Such as Family Homes, Heirlooms, and Businesses?

If you want to measure a person's true character, share an inheritance with him.
—Benjamin Franklin

Like the baby in the biblical story involving King Solomon, certain things cannot be divided without being destroyed. Suppose, for example, that a widow with three daughters owns a sterling silverware service for 12. The service has been in the family for many years, and the widow wishes to pass it on to the next generation. Divvying the silverware up equally among her three daughters will destroy the set while leaving each daughter with a largely useless service for four. A rare stamp or coin collection presents a similar situation: the whole is greater than the sum of its parts. Partitioning the set or collection wipes out the lion's share of its value.

You cannot divide the indivisible. But, as what follows illustrates, there are ways to pass such things on intact while doing your best to achieve justice and to promote family harmony.

Heirlooms and Jewelry

Suppose the mother in the previous example has several valuable items: the set of silverware, jewelry, rings, bracelets, necklaces, earrings, broaches, and so on. All are valuable, but some more so than others. What can the mother do now to minimize unfairness and resentment?

Specifying in Advance

If the mother had her own wishes as to which daughter should inherit the silverware, she can so provide in her Will (or in some states, in a written, signed, and dated memorandum attached to the Will). In such cases, however, she should consider providing money or other assets to her remaining daughters equal in value to the silverware.

The mother could also ask her children what heirlooms, items of jewelry, paintings, furniture, and so on, they would particularly desire to inherit. She could then do her best to accommodate these desires in her Will, or, if state law permits, in the memorandum. This memorandum can be changed from time to time. But bear in mind that the memorandum can only cover "personal property" and may not govern the transfer of "real property," such as homes or fixtures.

Appraisal Followed by Rotating Selections

One way to divide heirlooms and/or other items of sentimental or cash value is to combine appraisals with a series of rotating selections. Here, each item is professionally appraised and each child is provided with a list of the values of all items. The children determine the order of selection by chance (roll of dice, selection of a high card). Assuming there were three children, the sequence would change with each round: 1-2-3; 2-3-1; 3-1-2. The rotation would continue for succeeding rounds. With each turn, the child can pick any item not previously selected, with the value of that item charged against his or her share. After all desired items have been selected, the values are totaled for each child. The unselected items are sold and the proceeds (together with other funds, if necessary) are used to equalize the total value each child receives.

Family Home

If more than one child wants to own the family home, a common solution requires each interested party to submit a written bid, with the house going to the highest bidder. The "winner" then pays each of the other children his/her respective proportionate share of the winning purchase price. For example, if there are three children and the top bid is $300,000, the winner should pay $100,000 to each of the other two children. The funds with which to pay the $200,000 could be raised by the winner placing a mortgage on the home. Thus, the winner has a $300,000 residence, which cost him or her only $200,000, and each of the other children has $100,000. The home is kept in the family, and each child is treated equivalently.

If only one child desires the family home, it should be appraised, and it should go to that child. However, the others should receive equal value of other assets. Obviously, if no child is interested in having the home, it should be sold and the net proceeds divided.

Family Vacation Home

Family vacation homes present a different situation. Often the children have fond memories of these vacation homes and the fun they had there. They would like their own children to enjoy the beach, the lake, or the mountains, as they did.

Transferring the Home to a Limited Liability Company (LLC)

One approach that the authors have used to keep the vacation home within a family while providing for its use by all family members involves transferring title to the vacation home to a limited liability company (LLC). An LLC is a legal entity (like a corporation) that is relatively inexpensive to establish. The LLC is governed by a document called an Operating Agreement. The Operating Agreement, which can be tailored to each family's specific circumstances, sets forth the relationship of the owners to each other within the LLC. For example, each of the children could be an equal owner of the LLC. The Operating Agreement would then set out a timesharing arrangement for each child and his or her family covering use during holidays, vacation seasons, and other periods. Each child who wanted to participate would be required to contribute his or her respective share of the expenses of maintenance, utilities, repairs, taxes, and so on. The Operating Agreement should include provisions for a buyout if any child wants to withdraw from the LLC, or in the event a third person acquires partial ownership in the LLC as the result of a divorce settlement, gift, or bequest.

If not all of the children are interested in the family vacation home, the family can use the equalizing procedures described with regard to the main family residence to see that the vacation home stays in the family while each child gets an equivalent share of the inheritance.

Family Business

Quite often the most valuable asset owned by a Decedent is the family business. Although one or more of the children may want to retain and to continue to operate the business, generally, it does not lend itself to a division in kind. The problem is further compounded because those children who are not interested in continuing the business should still receive their pro-rata share of its value.

Arranging for management succession in a family business is the work of many years, and the topic deserves a book (or books) in its own right. If all of the children are not actively engaged in the business, we strongly recommend that *only* those who are actively engaged be permitted to retain an ownership interest. The financial interests of the children not actively engaged must be bought out. This will require that the value of the business as a going entity be professionally determined. Typically, the Decedent's Will or Trust Agreement, or the governing documents of the business itself, will identify the persons and method by which to carry out the valuation.

We recommend that non-active heirs of the Decedent be bought out because family run businesses, by nature, generate conflicts of interest virtually guaranteed to create serious problems. For example, the active owners will expect reasonable compensation for their services and will resent working hard to make the business successful for the benefit of "absentee owners." The non-active members (the absentee owners) will resent the salaries, bonuses, automobiles, and other "perks" paid to their siblings and will want a present return on their ownership interests. However, the payment of dividends may not be advisable for financial or tax reasons.

> *If all of the children are not actively engaged in the business, we strongly recommend that only those who are actively engaged be permitted to retain an ownership interest.*

The purchase of the interests of the non-active owners need not take place in one fell swoop. Typically, the buyout will take place in installments, which usually do not exceed five years. The obligation to make the installment payments should be evidenced by an interest bearing promissory note, which can be guaranteed personally by the active owners and possibly secured with assets of the business.

The children who desire to continue the business should have a Buy-Sell Agreement among themselves in order to provide an orderly procedure in the event of the voluntary withdrawal or death of any of them. Also, there should be reasonable restrictions placed against the transfer of ownership interests to other persons.

Question 10

Who Should Be My Executor or Trustee?

Love all, trust a few.
—Shakespeare

Some Basic Terms

Executors and Trustees are sometimes generically referred to as "Fiduciaries." A Fiduciary has control over property belonging to some other person(s) and is expected to manage that property for his or their benefit. The word "Fiduciary" derives from the Latin word meaning "faithful." In theory, the Fiduciary is supposed to serve with the utmost faithfulness. In practice, you need to have the utmost faith in a person before naming him or her your Executor or Trustee.

The Wills and Estates area commonly involves the following kinds of Fiduciaries:

Type of Fiduciary	When Involved
Executor (in some states called the "Personal Representative")	Appointed by a Testator's Will
Administrator	Appointed by a Probate Court where there is no Will, or the Will fails to name an Executor/Personal Representative
Trustee	Appointed by (1) a Grantor's Trust Agreement (Living Trust); or (2) Testator's Will (Testamentary Trust), where the Will establishes a Trust.

For the purposes of this Chapter, we assume you are establishing a Will or Trust and need to appoint a Fiduciary or Fiduciaries. It is permissible in all states to name more than one person to serve as Co-Fiduciaries of either a Will or a Trust. When naming more than one person, you need to consider not only how well the skills and knowledge of each person fit with the others, but also how well their personalities will allow them to work together.

Executors/Personal Representatives

The principal duties of an Executor are to:

1. locate and take control of the Decedent's assets (to "marshal" the assets)
2. pay the just debts of the Decedent
3. file income and estate tax returns, as required
4. distribute the remaining assets in accordance with the provisions of the Will.

Depending upon the amount and nature of the assets, the Executor's duties can be relatively simple, extremely complex, or somewhere in between.

Whom should you appoint to assume these responsibilities?

Someone Familiar With Your Assets and Affairs

Ideally, the person named should have some familiarity with the Decedent's assets and affairs, since an attorney can be hired to deal with legal and tax matters. The surviving spouse is, therefore, almost always named as the Executor, or as a Co-Executor.

> *Depending upon the amount and nature of the assets, the Executor's duties can be relatively simple, extremely complex, or somewhere in between*

Offspring as Co-Executor

One of the Decedent's offspring often serves as Co-Executor(s) with the surviving parent, particularly if that parent is elderly or infirm. This is usually a child who: has legal or business experience; is responsible by nature; and/or lives in the same area where the Probate proceedings take place. When considering how many Co-Executors to appoint, remember that more is not necessarily better. Multiple Co-Executors complicate paperwork. If relationships among Co-Executors are not good, fights—and costly litigation—frequently result.

Designate Successor Executors

Because life is uncertain, the Will should designate successor Executors to serve if the original designee(s) resigns, becomes disabled, or dies while the Estate is being probated. A more recent approach is to have the Will authorize the Executor to designate his or her own successor. This approach offers great flexibility in meeting unanticipated situations. However, it also opens the door to the appointment of persons whom the Decedent never would have selected.

Corporate Fiduciaries

Because tax laws and financial markets have become so complex, naming a Trust Company as a Fiduciary often makes sense. Today, most commercial banks have Trust Departments, which serve as Fiduciaries. If you have good relations with the bank where you conduct your financial affairs, you should ask to meet with the Trust Officers. Keep in mind, however, that the personnel in Trust Companies, as in any industry, come and go. Consequently, it is the reputation and financial solidarity of the institution more than the engaging personality of an individual that should be your guide. Also, your attorney, or accountant, has probably dealt with several corporate Fiduciaries and can make helpful recommendations. Corporate Fiduciaries generally understand Probate proceedings thoroughly. Such Fiduciaries keep careful records and know how to prepare income-tax and estate-tax returns. However, we recommend against naming a corporate Fiduciary as **sole** Fiduciary. Having a family member (that is, surviving spouse or child) as a Co-Fiduciary adds an important "personal" element to decision making. The death of a loved one involves tremendous emotional loss. There is psychological benefit to the family from having one of its members directly participate in the administration of the Estate.

How Selection of an Executor Affects Fees

State statutes entitle Executors and their attorneys to fees based upon the value of the assets being administered. These statutory fees are "minimum" fees with "sliding percentages." The percentages decrease as the value of the assets increase. A typical example is:

5% of the value of the first $5,000

4% of the value of the next $20,000

3% of the value of the next $75,000

2¾% of the value of the next $300,000

2½% of the value of the next $600,000

2% on all amounts over $1,000,000

However, if the administration of the Estate requires extraordinary services, the Executor and attorney can petition the Probate Court for additional fees. On the other hand, where the Will names an attorney as an Executor, the attorney cannot collect one fee for acting as the Executor and a second fee for acting as the attorney: "double-dipping" is forbidden.

Where the Executor is the surviving spouse or a child, and he or she is also the Beneficiary of the Estate, the Will often provides that the family member shall serve without compensation. The reason is that fees paid to a Fiduciary are subject to ordinary income tax while an inheritance is **not** subject to income tax. From a tax perspective, it can therefore make more sense to transfer the money as an inheritance than a fee. From a family-harmony perspective, where some, but not all, children are named as Fiduciaries, avoiding payment of fees to the Fiduciary children can avoid jealousies and resentments.

How Selection of an Executor Affects the Fidelity Bond

As discussed in Question 2, the Probate Court will require the Executor to post a bond in an amount equal to the value of the Estate assets. If the Testator has complete faith in the named Fiduciary, however, he or she can waive the bond requirement in the Will, thus saving bonding costs (see Question 2). The Probate court will also usually waive the bonding requirement if the Executor is a Trust Company with substantial net worth.

Trustees

Whereas an Executor serves only during the administration of the Estate, (usually a maximum of 18-24 months), a Trustee can serve for years. Further, while the duties of an Executor are basically administrative and ministerial in nature, a Trustee usually enjoys broad discretionary powers. Among the principal duties of a Trustee are investment and management of Trust assets. The nature of these assets (that is, stocks, real estate, a family business, and so on) will therefore determine the skills and knowledge to look for in selecting a Trustee or Co-Trustees.

Need for Business Experience and Understanding of Family

Careful investment and management requires financial acumen. Also, because Trusts frequently last for several years (or even decades), accurate record keeping is essential. For these reasons, at least one Trustee should have business experience. This function is sometimes best served by a Trust Company.

As noted previously, avoid appointing a Trust Company as sole Fiduciary. Too frequently, when a Trust Company is sole Trustee, the beneficiaries have to fight Trust Company officers to authorize payment for things such as summer camps, vacations for family members, a new car, or a condominium for a widow. Also, it is widely known in the legal community that a Corporate Fiduciary named as the Fiduciary for a Will or Trust will likely engage the attorney who drafted the instrument. (This practice creates an incentive for attorneys to recommend the Corporate Fiduciary.) This practice can also lead to conflict between the family and the Corporate Fiduciary if the family desires that another attorney be engaged. Typically, such conflict arises when family members are unhappy with the terms of the Trust. Family members invariably blame the attorney who drafted the Trust Agreement (and secured his position as Trust attorney) rather than the Grantor, who was their spouse, or parent.

One way to make sure the Trust Company remembers that Trust funds should benefit the family and not the Trust Company (or its attorney) is to have the surviving spouse (or a child) serve as a Co-Trustee. Another way is for the Trust Agreement to empower a majority of the income beneficiaries to replace the existing Corporate Trustee with a new one. It is amazing how accommodating a Corporate Trustee can become when threatened with removal (and loss of Trustee fees).

When an Attorney Should be a Co-Trustee

In many cases, the Grantor has come to rely upon and trust an attorney. Often, this attorney has represented the Grantor in business dealings through the years and may have become a confidant in personal matters as well. The Grantor therefore wishes the attorney to continue serving and protecting his interests after the Grantor's death.

> *A Corporate Fiduciary named as the Fiduciary for a Will or Trust will most likely engage the attorney who drafted the instrument.*

Unfortunately for the Grantor, the Trustees cannot be required by the Trust Agreement or Will to hire a specific attorney to provide legal services. As a result, the only way for the Grantor to ensure the attorney's ongoing involvement is to name the attorney a Co-Trustee.

Question 11

How Should Pension and Retirement Benefits Figure Into My Estate Planning?

A penny saved is a penny earned.
—Benjamin Franklin

There are a number of retirement-savings options available to you. To promote your own comfortable retirement and to help provide for the loved ones you will leave behind, you should take the following into consideration when crafting your estate plan:

Social Security Benefits

Level of Benefits

Your level of benefits is calculated based on the 35 years in which you reported the highest income on your income tax returns. On average, your income from Social Security will only be about 40 percent of whatever your income was at the time you retired, up to a certain maximum.

The "full" retirement age shifts from year to year, gradually inching up from what used to be age 65 to what will be 67 years old for Americans born in 1960 or later. You can retire early, currently age 62, but you will receive a reduced benefit amount for the duration of your lifetime as the price for retiring early. On the other hand, the longer you delay applying for benefits after age 67, the greater your benefits. You can use a computer program that calculates benefits at *www.ssa.gov.*

If you are married, there may be an additional benefit. If your spouse's benefits would be less than 50 percent of yours, your spouse will be bumped up to receive 50 percent of your benefits.

Who Is Entitled to My Benefits When I Die?

Federal law, and not your Will or Trust, determines who receives your benefits when you die.

If you die single, with no minor children, and you never had a marriage that lasted 10 years or longer, then your family or heirs receive none of your benefits, and the money you paid in Social Security taxes simply goes back into the system.

> *If you die single, with no minor children, and you never had a marriage that lasted 10 years of longer, then your family or heirs recieve none of your benefits.*

Surviving Spouse (Who Has Not Remarried)

If you had a marriage that lasted at least 10 years, then you and your ex-spouse became "vested" in each other's benefits, meaning each ex-spouse, as long as he or she has not subsequently remarried, can be eligible to receive benefits based upon the ex-spouse's Social Security contributions. Having an ex-spouse who is eligible to claim benefits from a prior marriage will not reduce the level of benefits otherwise available to your current spouse or children.

If your surviving spouse is caring for a child of yours who is a minor, then the surviving spouse starts to receive Social Security

73

benefits immediately. Otherwise, full retirement age for a spouse—meaning, the age that person can start receiving your benefits—is age 67 for those born after 1962, and between ages 65 and 67 for those born before 1962; however, the surviving spouse can elect to receive a reduced benefits package at age 60.

Minor or Disabled Children

If you leave a minor child but no surviving spouse when you die, then that minor child receives a percentage of your benefits. An adult child who is not disabled is not eligible to receive benefits as a result of your death.

Pension Plans

Most large and medium-sized companies offer a retirement pension plan to their employees. The traditional plan for many years was called a "defined *benefit* plan," meaning that, once you were eligible for the plan, you qualified for a certain benefit. The level of benefits is usually based on your age, your years of service with the company, and how much you were earning when you were working.

As the workforce has become more fluid, the "defined *contribution* plan," has become more prominent. As the name implies, the benefits are not defined by your years of service to a specific company, but by how much you (and perhaps your employer) contribute into it and how well those contributions have been managed.

Applicable law and the terms of the plan itself will determine what happens if you leave the company and what payments are made to your loved ones when you die. Typically, a widow/widower or minor children might receive some benefits, but not adult children or other relatives.

401(k) Account

How a 401(k) Account Works

The most well-known type of defined contribution plan is called a 401(k) plan, named after the section of the tax code that authorizes it.

Most 401(k) plans offer the participants an opportunity to invest in one or more among a selected group of mutual funds. Many employers will "match" your contributions, contributing a certain amount for every dollar you contribute yourself, usually up to a certain limit.

The major advantage is the potential for tax-free growth of your investment. Funds contributed by you are deducted directly from your paycheck: they are "pre-tax" and do not show up on your W-2 or 1099 at tax-time. You do not pay income tax on those dollars (or the interest, dividends, and capital gains they generate) until you take them out of the plan, years or decades later. Generally speaking, you cannot access the funds put into your 401(k) account until you are at least 59 1/2 years old without incurring a penalty for early withdrawal.

Certain people who work for public institutions are eligible to enroll in a "403(b)" plan instead, which in many ways is similar to a 401(k) plan.

Who Inherits My 401(k) Account When I Die?

A beneficiary designation form filled out when you opened your account directs how funds in the account will be distributed when you die. Your 401(k) Beneficiary designation *must* name your spouse, if you have one, as the primary beneficiary, unless he or she consents in writing to your naming somebody else. Assuming your spouse is the Beneficiary, he or she can then roll the account over into his or her own IRA (see the following section).

Whenever you make a Will or Trust, have your lawyer contact the administrator of your 401(k) to fill out a new Beneficiary designation, consistent with the Will or Trust.

Individual Retirement Account (IRA)

What Is an IRA?

An Individual Retirement Account (IRA) resembles a 401(k), except it is set up privately through a financial institution instead of through your employer. Anyone can decide to set up an IRA; there is no need to have your employer sponsor a plan, or to wait until you qualify to enroll in the company's plan. Like a 401(k), you have input into what types of investments your IRA makes.

Many IRAs are "rolled over" from a different account, either a 401(k) account of an employee who is no longer eligible to participate in the company's pension plan (perhaps because of resignation or termination), or from a different IRA, such as one inherited from a spouse. The timeframe for rolling over the previous account into a new IRA in your name may vary, so consult an expert without delay if you think you qualify for rollover.

The amount you can contribute to your IRA is limited to $4,000 per year, or $5,000 if you are over 50 and trying to "catch up" with your retirement needs. Like the money in a 401(k) plan, funds in an IRA grow tax-free. Although the contributions are not directly deducted from your paycheck, the money contributed may be deducted from your next income tax return and is, therefore, not taxed when contributed.

> *There is no need to have your employer sponsor an IRA, or to wait until you qualify to enroll in the company's plan.*

Who Inherits My IRA When I Die?

Similar to the 401(k) account described earlier, when you open your IRA account, you will fill out a Beneficiary designation form, which will dictate where the funds go when you die. The primary Beneficiary of your IRA account does not need to be your spouse, but if you live in a state that uses the "community property" system of tracking marital assets, your spouse will automatically have certain rights to your account. If you elect to name somebody other than your spouse as the primary Beneficiary, you should have your spouse register his or her consent by signing the Beneficiary designation form.

What are a Roth IRA and a Roth 401(k)?

A Roth IRA is an alternative form of IRA available to those making under a certain level of income, currently around $110,000 for a single person, $160,000 for a married couple. The money contributed to your Roth IRA will come from after-tax dollars, meaning they are not tax-deductible when you contribute them to the Roth IRA. But once contributed, the funds can grow free of tax until you withdraw them from the account. You can withdraw the funds in the IRA at any time without penalty. Likewise, there is also no requirement that you withdraw the funds at a minimum retirement age.

The flexibility and popularity of the Roth IRA has led to the creation, as of January 2006, of the Roth 401(k). This is a hybrid between the Roth IRA and a standard 401(k) defined contribution plan. The Roth 401(k) has the contribution limits of the 401(k), without the minimum salary requirements of the Roth IRA. Only after-tax dollars can be contributed to the Roth 401(k).

Question **12**

When Do I Need to Worry About Federal Estate Taxes?

In this world nothing is certain but death and taxes.
—Benjamin Franklin

The Estate and Gift Tax laws were enacted in the early 1900s to break up the fortunes of industrial dynasties like the Vanderbilts and Rockefellers. Over time, its reach has extended well into the middle class, as persons who were by no means wealthy found that the aggregate value of their parents' home, savings, insurance and other assets were enough to trigger taxes as high as 60 percent.

Exempt Amount and Rates

Estate Tax is imposed on the amount by which assets of an Estate exceed a specified value. *In this regard, please note that the "Estate" for Estate Tax purposes is a separate concept from the "Estate" for Probate purposes.* The Estate Tax definition will pull into the "Estate" many assets that do not form part of the "Probate Estate."

Currently, an Estate is subject to tax on its value in excess of $2,000,000. In effect, a person's "Gross Estate" (see chart that follows) is currently exempt from Estate Tax if the Gross Estate does not exceed $2,000,000 (the "Exempt Amount"). The law presently exempts the following amounts from Estate Tax, and imposes the following tax rates on any assets in excess of these amounts:

Calendar Year	Exempt Amount (value up to which no Estate Tax is imposed (per person))	Tax Rate on value of Estate that exceeds the Exempt Amount
2006-2008	$2,000,000	46% /45% /45%
2009	$3,500,000	45%
2010	Unlimted	No tax imposed
2011 and thereafter	$1,000,000	50%

Legislation presently before Congress would eliminate the Estate Tax completely and forever. However, most Estate Tax professionals believe that after much debate and rancor, Congress will ultimately retain the Estate Tax, but will raise the Exempt Amount, per person, to $3,500,000 to $5,000,000

The Gift Tax statutes were enacted to discourage the voluntary transfer of ownership of assets during lifetime that would result in (a) the reduction in income tax liability from high-bracket taxpayers to lower-bracket taxpayers, and (b) a reduction in the value of assets includible in the Gross Estate at death.

However, not all gifts will incur a Gift Tax liability. There is an annual exemption of $12,000, per person, for each person to whom gifts are made, and there is no limit on the number of donees. In addition, each taxpayer has a $1,000,000 lifetime exemption that can be utilized in varying amounts, from time to time, or can be totally used at one time. The mechanics, use, and application of these exemptions are explained, in detail, in the next chapter. If Gift Taxes are payable, the rates are the same as the Estate Tax rates.

Determining the Gross Estate

A federal Estate Tax return (Form 706) must be filed if a Decedent's "Gross Estate" exceeds the applicable Exempt Amount, even if no taxes may be due.

The starting point in calculating the Gross Estate is to determine the value of all property "owned" by the Decedent as of his or her Date of Death. All literally means all: cash, investments, business interests, real estate, jewelry, automobiles, and any other asset you can think of.

Then things get complicated. The term "owned" means not just "owned" in the straightforward sense of the word but also covers certain transfers or other transactions in which the Decedent retained an interest in, or an involvement with, any property. This can even include cases in which the Decedent did not keep title to the property. If a parent "gave" assets to a child with the understanding (actual or implicit) that parent would continue to receive income (dividends, interest, rents) from these assets, they would be included in the parent's Gross Estate.

The Gross Estate also includes certain transfers within three years before the Decedent's death if the transfer was made without receiving full and fair payment in exchange. The most common type of transfers which result in the "claw back" are transfers of life insurance policies and transfers to a Trust where the Decedent retained some benefit or control. In effect, this rule pulls certain gifts made within the three-year period before death back into the Gross Estate.

Revocable Trusts

We have previously discussed the advantage of using Revocable Living Trusts to avoid Probate (see Question 3). If a Grantor establishes a Living Trust and transfers his property to the Trust during his life, but reserves the right in the Trust Agreement to receive income or principal from the Trust, or to alter, amend, or revoke the Trust, the full value of the assets held by the Trust at the time of the Grantor's death will be included in his or her Gross Estate.

> *The Gross Estate also includes certain transfers within three years before the Decedent's death if the transfer was made without receiving full and fair payment in exchange.*

Life Insurance Proceeds

Where the Decedent had any "incident of ownership" in the policy, the proceeds are includable in her or her Gross Estate. An "incident of ownership" would include the right to name or change Beneficiaries, the right to borrow against the policy, or the right to make decisions regarding use of policy dividends. This rule not only captures a typical individual policy, but also most Group Term Life Insurance, because the employee usually has the right to name the Beneficiary.

Profit Sharing, Pension and 401(k) Plans, and IRAs

The Estate Tax laws provide that upon the death of a person who is a participant in a Retirement Plan (whether or not he or she has commenced receiving distributions prior to death), the full value of the Retirement Plan is included in the participant's Gross Estate. In most cases, "Retirement Plans" include Profit Sharing Plans, Pension Plans and 401(k) Plans ("Retirement Plans"). IRAs owned by a Decedent are, also, includible in the Gross Estate.

Joint Interests in Property

If the Decedent was joint owner of property, the measure of includability in the Gross Estate depends upon whether or not the other joint owner was the Decedent's surviving spouse. If the property were owned by the Decedent and his or her spouse, whether as tenants by the entireties or joint tenants with the right to survivorship, 1/2 of the value of the property would be included in the Decedent's Gross Estate. This is true irrespective of which of them paid for the property, or the respective percentages of their individual contributions.

However, if the joint owner is not the surviving spouse, then the amount to be included in the Decedent's Gross Estate is *the total value* of the property, *unless* the surviving joint owner can establish that he/she contributed to the acquisition cost. If the facts establish that both joint owners contributed to the cost of acquisition of the property, the respective percentages of the total acquisition cost must be determined. The value of the property at the time of the Decedent's death is then multiplied by the Decedent's respective contribution percentage and the result is the amount included in the Decedent's Gross Estate. The formula can be illustrated with the following example: a Decedent and his brother purchased a building for $500,000; the Decedent contributed $300,00 and the brother can prove that he contributed $200,000. The building is worth $800,000 at the time of Decedent's death. Because the brother can establish that he contributed 40 percent of the acquisition cost, only 60 percent of the $800,000, or $480,000, will be included in the Decedent's Gross Estate. Because the initial assumption is of total includability, we cannot over emphasize the importance of maintaining accurate records when property is acquired in joint names other than by a husband and wife.

If the Decedent received the property as a gift or inheritance along with other persons, the amount to be included in his/her Gross Estate at the time of death is his or her percentage share of the ownership multiplied by the total value of the property. For example, if three siblings inherited an apartment building from their parents and the building is worth $750,000 when the

Decedent sibling dies, the Gross Estate will include $250,000, or one-third of the value of the building.

An Exception to the Date-of-Death Rule for Valuing Assets

Throughout this Chapter, we have stated that the key valuation date is the Decedent's date of death ("DOD"). However, there is an exception to this basic rule. The Personal Representative may elect to value all of the assets in the Gross Estate as of the date which is six months after DOD if, and only if, the effect of using this alternative valuation date results in a *lower* Gross Estate. The Personal Representative cannot pick and choose which assets are valued at DOD and which are valued at the six-month date. If any asset is sold, exchanged, or disposed of between the DOD and the six-month date, the value as of the date of sale, exchange, or disposition must be used if the six-month date is used for valuing the remaining assets. Otherwise, the DOD value is used, and if an asset is sold during administration, an income tax gain or loss will be incurred.

Deductions From the Gross Estate

The facts that the Decedent's Gross Estate exceeds the Exempt Amount and that an Estate Tax Return must be filed do not automatically mean that estate taxes are payable. Certain deductions are authorized, which may reduce the Gross Estate. These deductions include the debts of the Decedent as of DOD, the expenses incurred in administering the estate (including probate court costs and fees), losses incurred during the estate administration, charitable contributions, and, possibly the most important for a married person, the marital deduction. After subtracting the previously mentioned deductions from the Gross Estate and adding back certain taxable gifts made by the Decedent, the Taxable Estate is determined. From this amount, the tax is initially calculated and then a "Unified Credit" is deducted from the tax. The application of the Unified Credit is, in essence, the procedure by which the Exempt Amount is excluded from taxation.

Question 13

What Are the Basics of Federal Estate-Tax Planning?

"Over and over again courts have said that there is nothing sinister in so arranging one's affairs as to keep taxes as low as possible."
—Judge Learned Hand,
Comm. vs Newman 159 F.2d 848, 850-51

If, after reading Question 12, you believe that some part of your Gross Estate may exceed the Exempt Amount and be subject to Estate Tax, what can you do about it?

Your options depend to a great degree on what kind of assets you own and whether you are married.

Make Gifts During Your Lifetime

One simple way to reduce the Gross Estate is to make gifts to children and grandchildren each year during your lifetime. Under federal Gift Tax law, which is closely linked to the Estate Tax, every year you can give up to $12,000 to *each* of as many persons ("Donees") as you wish. The federal Gift Tax refers to this $12,000 per-person amount as the "Annual Exclusion." A married couple acting together can give twice as much, or $24,000, even if all of the money comes from the pockets of one spouse.

Where a Donee receives more than $12,000 in any one year, each spouse who contributed to the gift should file a Gift Tax return. If there are several children and grandchildren, during a period of years these gifts can substantially reduce the Donor's Gross Estate.

> *Where a Donee receives more than $12,000 in any one year, each spouse who contributed to the gift should file a Gift Tax return.*

The tax laws will only recognize gifts if they are "completed." The Donor must part with all interest in, and control over the asset. The Donee must obtain present use and enjoyment of the asset. This is referred to as a "present interest." Highly technical or counter-intuitive rules can arise where gifts to Trusts or minors are concerned. Seek expert advice.

Unlimited Gifts to Grandchildren For Educational or Medical Purposes

A grandparent may further reduce his or her Gross Estate by making tuition and medical payments for the benefit of his or her grandchildren. These payments, if made *directly* to the educational institution, or the medical services provider, are *not* subject to the Annual Exclusion limitation and so won't trigger any Gift Tax.

$1,000,000 Lifetime Gift Exemption

In addition to the Annual Exclusion, each person has a Lifetime Gift Exemption of $1,000,000. In practical terms, the Lifetime Gift Exemption functions as an exemption account of $1,000,000 against which certain large gifts can be credited. For example, assume a widow makes a gift of $25,000 to her daughter. The first $12,000 is treated as the Annual Exclusion; the balance of $13,000 is charged against the Lifetime Gift Exemption. Thus, even though the gift exceeded the Annual Exclusion, no tax is payable because of the Lifetime Gift Exemption. However, that Exemption has now been reduced to $987,000 ($1,000,000 minus $13,000). If the Donor is married, the amount of any gift in excess of $24,000, per year, will be charged equally against the Lifetime Gift Exemption of each spouse.

Don't Let the Tail Wag the Dog

There is an adage that "one father can raise seven sons, but seven sons can't support one father." In theory, almost everyone could avoid or greatly reduce Estate Taxes by transferring property to his or her children and grandchildren prior to death. In practice, elderly people rightly hesitate to surrender their financial independence by giving away their wealth to their children without knowing what the future may hold.

So be practical about what you'll need to live on in your old age, and hang onto it. Don't let your dislike of paying taxes upset your judgment, your peace of mind or your own enjoyment of your "golden years."

Combine the Exempt Amount and the Marital Deduction

The Estate and Gift Tax permits you to make unlimited gifts to your spouse free of Gift Tax. You can also leave your spouse an unlimited amount of money or other assets when you die free of Estate Tax. This tax-free treatment is known as the "Marital Deduction."

Probably the most important estate-planning concept for a married couple is to combine the Exempt Amount for each spouse with the unlimited Marital Deduction when the first spouse dies. The benefits of this combination can be seen through the following examples:

Example 1: Results Without Combining—$900,000 of Tax

Assume a married couple has assets worth $4,000,000, which are held in joint names. If the husband dies in 2006, his Gross Estate will be $2,000,000 because of the joint ownership (see Question 12). No Estate Tax will be due, however, because his Gross Estate does not exceed the $2,000,000 Exempt Amount in 2006.

Because all of the assets were held in joint names, though, the widow becomes the sole owner of everything upon her husband's death. If she were to die in 2008, the $4,000,000 would be included in her Gross Estate. Because the Exempt Amount is scheduled to remain at $2,000,000 in 2008, her estate would then owe Estate Tax on the other $2,000,000, which at the 45 percent rate would be *$900,000*.

Example 2: Results With Combining—$0 of Tax

Proper tax planning can avoid this $900,000 tax burden without hurting the couple's living standard while both are alive; in addition, all of the funds can remain available for the widow after her husband's death (assuming for the purposes of the example that he is the first to die).

The key factor is to keep the husband's share of the assets out of the widow's Gross Estate when she dies.

Planning Steps

Step One is to separate the joint ownership so that the husband and wife *each* own assets worth $2,000,000.

Next, the husband and wife each transfer his or her assets to a Revocable Living Trust. Each is the Beneficiary of his or her own Trust during his or her life. Under the terms of each Trust, when the initial Beneficiary dies, the surviving spouse, for the rest of his or her life, will receive the income from the late spouse's trust. However, the successor Trustee does *not* elect to have the Trust qualify for the Marital Deduction. When the survivor dies, each Trust will terminate, and the assets will be distributed to their children.

Planning Consequences

Because the couple are the Beneficiaries of their own Trusts, the couple continues to enjoy the income from the $4,000,000.

Because the husband's Trust was worth $2,000,000, the husband's Exempt Amount avoids Estate Tax. Moreover, because these assets remain in Trust and were never qualified for Marital Deduction, they are not included in the widow's Gross Estate upon her death. Thus, upon the widow's death in 2008, *only* her Trust is included in her Gross Estate. Because the value of her Trust is covered by the $2,000,000 Exempt Amount, no Estate Tax is due.

Key Takeaway: Make Full Use of the Exempt Amount

In almost all situations where a married couple owns substantial assets, each should own assets in his or her individual name at least equal to the applicable Exempt Amount. A major oversight in estate planning is the failure to utilize this concept. This failure becomes particularly costly when a wife, who had few assets in her own name, predeceases her husband, who owns substantial assets in his name. Her Estate loses the benefit of passing assets equal to the Exempt Amount tax-free to the children (directly or via a Non-Marital Deduction Trust).

Because the Marital Deduction also applies to lifetime gifts between spouses, it would be advisable for the husband to make gifts to his wife, or to a Marital Trust for her benefit, so that the Exempt Amount will be utilized if she were to die first. If gifts are made for the purpose of utilizing the Exempt Amount, it is critical to make sure that if the donee-spouse dies first, the assets are not bequeathed to the donor-spouse.

To Trust or Not to Trust

To qualify for the Marital Deduction, the law only requires that the assets go to the surviving spouse. The law does not require that this transfer be via a Trust. But, we believe that using a Trust best protects the financial interests of the couple's children and grandchildren.

Leaving assets outright to the surviving spouse raises the risk that a gold-digger, gigolo, or other person (relative or outsider) will divert the money. A Marital Deduction Trust can prevent this diversion of assets. But, to qualify for the Marital Deduction, the Trust *must* provide that all income of the Trust be paid to the surviving spouse, at least annually, for his or her life. There cannot be any contingencies or conditions limiting the surviving spouse's right to all of the income for life. Although not required as a condition to qualify for the Marital Deduction, we suggest that the Trustee be given discretion to utilize principal for the surviving spouse's benefit in special situations (that is, illness, accident, misfortune). To further protect the assets from unintended "Beneficiaries," we suggest that the surviving spouse not serve as sole Trustee of the Marital Trust. An adult child should be a Co-Trustee (See Question10).

Upon the death of the surviving spouse (whether remarried, or not) the entire balance of the assets are distributed to the descendants in accordance with the wishes of the spouse who created the Trust. Because family situations can change dramatically between the death of the first spouse and the death of the surviving spouse, it may be wise to give the surviving spouse some rights to adjust the ultimate distributions among the descendants. The Trust Agreement can give the surviving spouse a "Limited Power of Attorney" to address matters that may have risen after the death of the first spouse (that is, a child's divorce, unexpected death, financial reverses, grandchild's special medical needs, and so on).

Question 14

How Should I Use Life Insurance to Protect My Loved Ones?

For man does not know his time
—Ecclesiastes 9:12

Why Life Insurance Is Different

You might drive a car for your entire life and never have an accident. A flood or fire may never damage your home. But one day, each of us will die. Life insurance differs from other types of insurance because if you keep your policy in force, the insurance company will eventually have to pay in full. The prices and types of life insurance therefore take into account not just the probability you will die within a certain period, but also the likelihood you will cancel your policy before you die.

We mention this difference because too often people focus on how much insurance they should buy without also thinking through:

⊃ what type(s) of life insurance they need

⊃ how they will pay for it in the long term.

Buying the wrong kind of insurance can leave you unable to afford it down the road when you need it most, or it can mean you spent years and years paying high premiums on insurance that you no longer need.

Some Basic Terms

An insurance policy is a contract between the insurance company and the policy Owner. It involves the following:

➲ The "Insured" is the person upon whose life the policy is based.

➲ The "Beneficiary" is the person who will receive the proceeds of the policy upon the death of the "Insured."

➲ The "Owner" is the person (or other entity) who has the right to name the "Beneficiary.

Frequently, the Owner and Insured are the same person. The Owner then designates a family member, or a Trust, as the Beneficiary. However, the Owner and Insured need not be the same person. For reasons discussed in Questions 3 and 13, we recommend that the Beneficiary be a Trust set up for the benefit of the surviving spouse and children. As discussed in Question 13, there are important estate tax considerations with respect to the designation of the Owner of the policy.

The payments of the premiums on the policy can be made by any person. If, however, the premiums are paid by someone other than the Owner, the premium payments may constitute gifts to the Owner or Beneficiaries.

Advantages of Life Insurance

Life insurance often represents the primary source of financial security should the family breadwinner die prematurely. Also, because a premature death of the homemaker may very well require the hiring of a housekeeper, nanny, and the like, young couples increasingly purchase insurance on the life of the homemaker as well.

To promote financial security (and to keep people off governmental assistance), federal and the state laws grant life insurance certain legal advantages. For example, benefits paid on a life insurance policy are exempt from ordinary income tax. Every state completely, or substantially, exempts life insurance proceeds from the reach of the deceased-Insured's creditors. Some portion of the cash value of the policy may be exempt from creditors of the Owner of the policy.

Where Do I Buy It?

Most people buy insurance through an agent, who receives a commission from the insurance company when you buy a policy. The Internet has also opened a new channel for buying insurance, either directly from the insurance companies themselves, from agents' Websites or from the Websites of so-called "aggregators," who will typically promise some kind of automated price-comparison to get you the best deal.

We recommend a combination of talking to agents and online comparison. Speak to at least two or three agents and compare the prices of what they recommend against what's available online. If the price is close, buy from the agent, assuming you're happy with the service he or she has given you. A good way to find a reputable agent is to ask your attorney, accountant, or banker; they have had experience dealing with several agents. We would strongly recommend that you select an agent who has the designation of "CLU," which means Chartered Life Underwriter. There are rigorous courses and tests which must be taken and passed for an agent to achieve the CLU designation. It is analogous to an accountant qualifying as a CPA.

How Much Do I Need?

Your stage in life will determine the amount of insurance you need.

Typically, you most need insurance when you are starting and raising a family. Your insurance needs will diminish once your children complete their educations. But, if the family has had a principal breadwinner, the breadwinner should plan on keeping a substantial policy in force for his or her entire life for the benefit of a surviving spouse.

With regard to specific amounts, insurance companies have suggested an amount equal to five times the family's annual income as a starting point. Obviously, this is an arbitrary number. You should take many factors into consideration:

- ➲ the age of your spouse and the number and ages of your children
- ➲ the amount of other assets you own
- ➲ mortgages and debts that are owed
- ➲ probabilities of inheritances from parents
- ➲ future prospects for increases in income
- ➲ funds available for premiums after paying for food, clothing, shelter, and so on.

Do not over-buy and then become resentful of paying premiums. All too often, when this occurs, the policy becomes a burden and is allowed to lapse.

What Kind Should I Buy?

There are basically three kinds of life insurance policies offered: (1) Term; (2) Ordinary Life (also called Whole Life); and (3) Universal Life.

Term

You can purchase term life insurance on a yearly basis just as you would purchase auto insurance. Term life insurance is the least expensive type of life insurance available. But, while your auto insurance premiums may remain relatively constant over time, the premiums for yearly—renewable—Term insurance will continue to escalate as you get older and the probability of your death increases.

A type of Term insurance that avoids the annual increase is a "Term Certain" policy. This policy will lock in the amount of the premium for a certain period, usually up to 20 years. However, at the end of the period, the policy terminates, and the insured has no residual benefit from the prior premiums paid.

For reasons mentioned previously, Term insurance (whether annual or Term Certain) is not a good policy for the very long term. In fact, only 2 percent of all term policies ever result in the payment of death benefits; 98 percent of the time, the policies are dropped or expire before the death of the Insured.

Whole Life (Also Called "Ordinary Life")

In the early years, Whole or Ordinary Life has the highest annual premiums for the coverage provided. However, these premiums remain the same for the insured's entire life and, so long as the premiums are paid, the policy never expires or terminates.

The reason for the higher premium is that the policy has a savings component known as the "cash value." Each year, a portion of the premium is credited by the insurance company to a savings account for the benefit of the Owner of the policy. The insurance company guarantees a minimum return on this account, usually 3 percent or 4 percent.

If the insurance company is a "mutual" company, the actual rate of return may exceed the guaranteed rate. In addition, mutual companies earn annual dividends for policy Owners.

The earnings on the savings accounts and the dividends from mutual companies are income-tax-free to the policy Owner. The Owner can:

1. Take the annual dividend in cash.
2. Contribute the dividend towards payment of the annual premium.
3. Buy additional insurance with the dividend.
4. Leave the dividend with the Company to earn interest.

The cash value of the policy is a fund of money that is always available to the Owner. If the owner elects, he or she can borrow the cash value ("Policy Loan") for as long as he or she desires. Interest will be payable annually and, upon the death of the Insured, the unpaid balance of the Policy Loan will be deducted from the death benefits paid by the company. If the Owner determines that he or she no longer wants the policy, he or she can simply cash out the policy.

Universal Life

Universal Life is a blend of Term Insurance and Whole Life. The premiums are higher than for Term insurance, but less than for Whole Life. When the Owner pays the annual premium, it is credited to an interest-bearing account. The company guarantees an interest rate of 3 percent or 4 percent, but if the company's investments perform well, you will earn additional interest, which can be used to pay the premiums.

Universal Life insurance is marketed on the assumption the company's investments will consistently return more than the guaranteed rate. If you are considering Universal Life, you must review projections based upon the *guaranteed* rate of return and not the "assumed" rate. These projections will show that, unless you pay substantially higher premiums in future years, the policy will lapse and terminate.

Some insurance companies have added a new feature to their Universal Life policies known as a "Secondary Guarantee." The Secondary Guarantee provides that if you pay a fixed annual premium for the life of the Insured, the policy will not lapse and the death benefit will be paid. In essence, a Universal Life policy with a Secondary Guarantee provision is a Whole Life policy with no cash-value features.

Mixing and Matching

We believe the best strategy for most people is a combination of: Term insurance plus Whole or Universal Life with a Secondary Guarantee. Buy a Whole Life policy for the very long term, that is, with the intent to keep it in force for the rest of your life. Then use Term insurance (whether annual Term or Term Certain) to carry you through the years you are raising your family.

Question 15

What Must I Do if I Am Getting Married or Remarried?

Marry in haste, repent at leisure.
—Anonymous

Innumerable books, magazine articles, and Websites will tell you how to find and win the heart of Mr./Ms. Right. Our advice is purely practical: know whom you're marrying. A surprising number of people make the most important commitment of their lives without finding out their intended's past, character, and values. Sadly, love does not conquer all, but foolishness often loses everything.

We expect the couple in question to ignore the previous advice. So, for readers who are friends or relatives, we suggest using the research tools available on the Internet to check on credit, criminal background, and the like. Don't think this doesn't apply because your friend's fiancé/e has no tattoos. The authors encountered one case where a woman married a professional at a prestigious accounting firm, only to discover he had a criminal conviction for forging a prescription, as well as a gambling problem.

Premarital Agreements

Premarital Agreements are not only for the super-rich. The laws governing these Premarital Agreements vary widely from state to state, but in all cases, such Agreements must be in writing and signed by both parties. We also advise that these Agreements be acknowledged in writing in the same manner as deeds of conveyance.

For a young couple marrying for the first time, a Premarital Agreement would likely enter the picture only if there were a family asset that people wished to stay in the family: shares in a family business, interest in a family home, and so on. With many people marrying later in life, however, one or both of the parties may have accumulated substantial assets they may wish to keep separate, at least for the first few years of marriage. As an alternative to a Premarital Agreement, the party with the asset might consider placing it in Trust to keep the asset as "Separate Property." (See Question 6.)

Separate Attorneys

Both parties to the Premarital Agreement should be represented by separate attorneys of his or her own selection. We further recommend that each attorney be required to sign the Agreement as a witness. This is not necessary to make the Agreement binding, but makes it very hard for either side's lawyer to claim later that he or she was not aware of what the client was signing or that the client signed it against the lawyer's advice.

Disclosure of Finances

The Premarital Agreement must disclose the assets and liabilities of each party. This ensures that each knows the financial position of the other before waiving any marital or elective rights to share in a spouse's property. Disclosure usually takes the form of a detailed balance sheet setting out a party's assets, liabilities, and net worth. The balance sheets of both

97

parties are then attached to the Agreement as Exhibits and made a part of the Agreement. Some states provide that if a full financial disclosure is made prior to the execution of the Premarital Agreement, a party will not need to make any reasonable financial provisions for the other in the event of a subsequent divorce or death.

No Agreement Is "Ironclad"

Even if you follow the previously described steps, there is no guarantee a Premarital Agreement will be enforced as written. Divorce courts seek "to do equity." This means doing what is fair and reasonable taking all of the circumstances into consideration notwithstanding the letter of an Agreement, or even the letter of the law. For example, where financial circumstances have changed dramatically after the Agreement is signed, a divorce court may find that these changes make the terms of the Agreement so unfair that the Court won't enforce the Agreement. (The legal term is "unconscionable.") In such cases, Courts have been known to award a party far more than the Agreement provides.

A useful maxim to bear in mind is: "pigs get fed; hogs get slaughtered." You are better off providing reasonably for your future spouse and thereby having an Agreement that will be enforced, than getting your future spouse to sign such a one-sided agreement that a court will be tempted to set it aside.

Rights to Benefits

If either party is employed by a Company that maintains a pension, profit sharing, or 401(k) retirement plan, a newly married employee should reconfirm the name of the Beneficiary of his or her retirement plan. In many situations, the plans designate a priority-list of Beneficiaries (that is, spouse, parent, children) if the employee fails to name a specific person. For example, we have been involved in litigation where a retirement plan designated a spouse as first Beneficiary, but a single man specifically named his mother as his Beneficiary. He then married but did not change the Beneficiary designation. He died, and both his mother and spouse fought for the substantial Benefits under the plan. The wife claimed that as a result of the marriage, she became the Beneficiary; the mother argued that the failure to make any change after the marriage indicated her son's desire that she continue as Beneficiary.

If the retirement plan is subject to the federal ERISA laws, a spouse is automatically the Beneficiary unless the spouse gives *written consent* for another person to be so designated. Please check with your respective employer to confirm that the persons designated as Beneficiaries of your retirement plans are those whom you want to receive the Benefits in the event of your death.

We also recommend that in connection with the marriage, the parties review the named beneficiaries of all their insurance policies and IRAs. Each spouse should also have a Will prepared to avoid disputes between a surviving spouse and his or her in-laws.

Remarriage

Remarriages do not inevitably result in adversarial relationships, but do require careful planning. In particular, where either party has children by a prior partner/spouse, Premarital Agreements and Trusts should be established. Keep in mind that if a party has substantial assets and remarries without a Premarital Agreement, then, upon that person's death, the surviving spouse will have substantial statutory rights to share in the estate (see Question 6).

For the sake of the following example, we assume below that a man with children by a prior marriage wishes to re-marry. The man wants to provide financial security for his new wife, but at the same time, he does not want the assets to be diverted to the new wife's children from a prior marriage, or to the new wife's next husband, should she survive the man and marry again. The man's wishes can be satisfied with a properly drafted Trust.

The Trust can be funded either before or at the time of the man's death with investment assets that will produce current income. The income will go to the widow in periodic (usually quarterly) installments to be used for her support, comfort, welfare, and maintenance. If the man so desires, he can authorize the Trustees to encroach upon the Trust principal in special circumstances, such as sickness, accident, misfortune, and so on. Upon the widow's death, the Trust terminates and the assets are distributed to the man's children from his first marriage (assuming he had no children by his widow). The widow will have no control over the final disposition of the assets.

If the Trust is to continue for the widow's lifetime and the income is payable to without limitations or conditions, the Trust (known as a "Q-Tip Trust") can qualify for a Marital Deduction in the man's Estate (see Question 13). This will defer Estate Taxes on the value of the assets in the Trust at the time of the man's death and thereby avoid a reduction of the income producing assets. The value of the Trust at the time of the widow's death will be included in the widow's Gross Estate. However, there may be no taxes payable if the Gross Estate falls within the then applicable Exemption Amount (see Question12). If so, the man's children will receive the Trust assets tax-free.

The foregoing plan depends upon the man's willingness to provide support for his widow for her lifetime. However, the man may believe that if his widow remarries, his obligation of support to her should cease. The Trust can be structured to terminate if the widow remarries. However, if it is possible that the Trust *may* terminate prior to the widow's death, it will **not** qualify for a Marital Deduction when the man dies. This is the case even if the widow never remarries and the Trust does not, in fact, terminate before her death.

There is a practical consideration to using the Trust arrangement for a second spouse. The children from the man's first marriage must wait until their stepmother dies before receiving those of their father's assets that were put into the Trust. The children may resent having to wait depending on:

- ➲ what other assets are owned by the children (or were bequeathed to them by their father)
- ➲ the widow's life expectancy

Consequently, before a lifetime Trust for a second spouse is established, the prospective Grantor should carefully evaluate his or her over-all financial situation and be aware of the likely effect the arrangement will have on his or her children.

Question 16

?

What Must I Do if I Am Getting Divorced?

> *I am a good housekeeper:*
> *when I divorce, I keep the house.*
> —Zsa Zsa Gabor

Approximately 50 percent of all marriages end in divorce; in addition, some couples elect a Legal Separation rather than formally divorcing.

Legal Separation

This arrangement has many of the trappings of a divorce: the parties physically separate; negotiate and execute a support agreement; arrange custody of children; often, the Separation Agreement includes provisions relating to a subsequent divorce.

Unfortunately, however, the couple frequently overlook what happens when one of them dies. Unlike a divorce, a Legal Separation will *not* preclude a separated spouse from claiming statutory benefits upon the death of the other spouse *unless* the written Separation Agreement specifically provides for a waiver or renunciation of such benefits.

Divorce

Although, in some States, a judicial termination of marriage is called a "marital dissolution," for simplicity, we will use the term "divorce."

Separate Property vs Marital Property

Next to a custody fight over children, the most bitter wrangling in a divorce proceeding concerns what is "Separate Property" and what is "Marital Property."

"Separate Property" includes assets owned by a person prior to his or her marriage and which remain in his or her individual name after the marriage. Separate Property also comprises individual gifts or property inherited during marriage. Wedding gifts are deemed to be given jointly to the couple on a 50/50 basis.

"Marital Property" includes all property acquired by either spouse during the marriage, except gifts and inheritances, and property acquired in exchange for Separate Property.

Failure to Keep Separate Property Separate

Placing *Separate Property* into joint names, or adding it to an account in joint names, makes the entire amount *Marital Property*. For example, if the husband inherits a sum of money from his wealthy uncle and deposits the money into a joint bank account with his wife, the inheritance is now Marital Property.

Even if Separate Property is held separately, income attributable to the Separate Property during the marriage is generally considered Marital Property. Moreover, if the spouse who originally owned the Separate Property cannot accurately trace the earnings from the original property, a divorce court may very well hold that it is all Marital Property. This result is even more likely if the earnings (dividends and interest) over the years were reported on joint income tax returns.

Another scenario where seemingly Separate Property may, in some States, become Marital Property is when a Separate Property asset increases in value during the marriage. All States agree that the value at the time of inheritance is Separate Property. However, States differ on how to treat the increase in value. Some States treat the amount of the increase as Separate Property while others treat the amount of the increase as Marital Property.

A good rule of thumb is to consider all property owned by the spouses as Marital Property, and if a party claims that certain assets are Separate Property, the burden of tracing and proving the status of Separate Property is on that party.

Dividing Marital Property

The divorce court determines whether assets are Separate Property or Marital Property. Assets deemed Separate Property must go entirely to the spouse who owns them. However, the court has discretion to divide Marital Property between the parties as the court deems fair (equitable) under all the circumstances.

In practice, courts consider the amount of Separate Property owned by each spouse in deciding how to divide the Marital Property. So, for example, if a husband owns $500,000 of Separate Property, and the wife owns $150,000 of Separate Property, and they jointly own $300,000 of Marital Property, a divorce court may award the wife more than one-half of the Marital Property so the two spouses end up with nearer the same amount of money.

Effect of a Spouse's Death on Separate Property

In non-community property States, absent a Premarital Agreement, the difference between Separate and Marital Property disappears upon the death of a spouse. The statutory and elective rights of a surviving spouse (see Question 6) will apply to the formerly Separate Property of the deceased spouse. Also, a transfer, without adequate consideration, of Separate Property by a spouse prior to his or her death may be deemed a transfer in fraud of the other spouse's marital rights. Such a transfer can be nullified.

In community property States, Separate Property owned prior to the marriage will retain its status as Separate Property after the marriage.

Effect of Divorce on Wills, Trusts, and Insurance Policies

Full or Partial Revocation of Wills

In a few States, a divorce has the effecting of revoking a Will entirely. In most States, however, a divorce only revokes those provisions for the benefit of the ex-spouse. The States are split as to whether a divorce automatically revokes any bequests to relatives of the ex-spouse, such as step-children or parents. The Uniform Probate Code, which has been adopted in several but not all States, does provide for a revocation of bequests to all relatives of the ex-spouse who are not also relatives of the Testator.

Effect on Assets in Trust, Insurance Policies Varies By State

Because of the increasing popularity of Revocable Living Trusts, we frequently find that such Trusts own the major percentage of a person's investment assets. Divorce courts treat assets held in Revocable Living Trusts as being owned by the Grantor. Thus, in dividing Marital Property, the value of the assets in a Revocable Living Trust are taken into consideration. It is essential that the Grantor of a Trust who is in the midst of a divorce proceeding seek legal advice as to whether his or her State provides the same revocation rule for the Trust as it does for a Will. If revocation is not automatic, the Grantor must amend the Trust to remove the ex-spouse as a Beneficiary or Trustee. In addition, the Beneficiary designations (usually the ex-spouse) of insurance policies and retirement plans and IRAs will have to be changed to remove the name of the ex-spouse.

> *In dividing Marital Property, the value of the assets in a Revocable Living Trust are taken into consideration.*

Joint Property

If property is owned by the spouses as tenants-by-the-entireties, or as JTWROS (see Question 3), a divorce acts as an automatic termination of survivorship rights. The property is deemed to be owned by the two parties as tenants-in-common, each with a 1/2 interest. Usually, the divorce decree, or Property Settlement Agreement, spells out how the property will be disposed of. In many cases, the property is sold, the mortgage, if any, is paid and the net proceeds are equally divided. In other situations, the entire property may be awarded to only one spouse and a financial adjustment made with other assets to reflect the value of the 1/2 interest being divested.

Life Insurance

Beneficiaries

A common situation in connection with a divorce is where the husband promises to keep the wife and children as the named Beneficiaries of his life insurance policies after the divorce. The promise may be oral, or it may be included in the Settlement Agreement.

Often, however, the ex-husband later remarries (or merely changes his mind) and replaces the original Beneficiaries with a new one. The ex-wife and children do not learn of their having been replaced until after the ex-husband's death. They then file suit against the husband's Estate, the new Beneficiary, and probably the insurance company to enforce the promise made at the time of the divorce. If the promise was oral, the ex-wife and children have a real uphill battle; if the promise was in writing, their case is much stronger.

To avoid a change of Beneficiaries and resulting litigation, the husband should be required to sign an "irrevocable designation of Beneficiary" form naming the wife and children and to file this form with the insurance company. Such an irrevocable designation prevents the ex-husband from changing the Beneficiary without the ex-wife's express, written consent.

Notice of Premium Payments

In addition, the ex-wife needs to make sure that she receives notice of premium payments. This way, if the ex-husband defaults on his obligation to keep the insurance in force, the ex-wife will have notice and an opportunity to cure the default and to maintain the policy in force. If the policy is one with cash value, the insurance contract usually contains a provision for the cash value to be used to pay the premiums rather than allow the policy to lapse.

When Is a House Not an Asset?

During a divorce, the emotional power of a home can cloud people's judgment. In many cases, the wife wants to retain the home to symbolize that her husband—and not she—is being expelled from the family.

Be careful. Husbands will often exploit a wife's emotional attachment to the family home to extract concessions in a divorce settlement. Also, homes can require a great deal of cash for mortgage payments, taxes, utilities, and maintenance. If the wife does not properly calculate—and get a property settlement that takes into account—the carrying costs of the house—it will turn quickly from an asset into a liability.

Question 17

Why Should I Give Money Now Rather Than After I Die?

The manner of giving is worth more than the gift.
—Pierre Corncille,
Le Menteur (1642)

The question whether to give money to one's children (or grandchildren) now or to bequeath it to them after death often has no easy answer. Parents naturally desire to help their children. At the same time, parents want to ensure their own financial security for retirement. (Expensive medical needs, such as nursing-home care, are a particular concern.) Moreover, parents must fight the urge to give with strings attached (the "golden umbilical cord"), as well as beware giving so freely that their children fail to develop responsibility and self-reliance (the "golden teat").

The Golden Umbilical Cord

Many successful business people believe they know best how to manage the money they have earned. All too often, they use this money to control their children. Gifts come with

109

strings attached; that is, "I will be generous provided that you do what I want." The child agrees to the control that comes with the gifts. Although the child complies with the parent's wishes, both the child and his or her spouse become resentful.

The Golden Teat

The reverse of the golden umbilical cord is giving money so freely that it retards the child's development as a fully functioning adult. This situation applies not only to rich trust-fund babies but to people of average means whose parents too frequently or readily bail them out of predicaments. Sometimes you have to temper the instinct to help with the realization that you may be funding and furthering habits and behavior that will only change when the child faces the full consequences of his or her own doings.

Practical Considerations for Giving Now

Two practical considerations in favor of giving now bear mentioning:

1. a smaller gift now can often do more good than a larger bequest later
2. some early gifting enjoys substantial income and Estate-tax benefits

Seed Money

An early gift is sometimes referred to as "seed money." An example might be a $25,000 gift by a parent to help a child buy a house now for a growing family. The gift would not only help provide a home, but allow the child to stop paying rent and to start building equity. Such a gift will likely deliver more benefit than an inheritance of a $100,000 years hence when the grandchildren have grown and moved out.

Seed money can also enable a child to start a business, or to participate in a venture he or she might otherwise have to pass-up. Of course, seed money need not always take the form of an outright gift, but can involve lending to or co-investing with the child on better terms than the child could get from a stranger.

Section 529 Gifts for Education

Grandparents frequently desire to provide funds for their grandchildren's education. Because of the rapidly rising costs of private schools and colleges, the sooner educational gifting (and investing) begins, the better.

Internal Revenue Code Section 529 provides unique income-tax benefits for money given to help pay for a child's or grandchild's education. The law permits the States to authorize financial institutions to create "Section 529 Plans." These Plans usually provide that individual investment accounts may be opened in the name of a minor and the accounts funded with gifts from parents or grandparents. Account funds can usually be invested in one or more mutual funds selected by the person who made the initial contribution (gift). In some States, the donor even receives an annual tax credit, limited in amount, for the contribution.

The dividends, interest, and capital gains earned by the account are *exempt* from income tax. Further, the funds withdrawn in later years to pay for the grandchild's college education are also exempt. Tax-free treatment of both the initial gift and investment income provides tremendous financial advantages over money given and invested outside of a 529 Plan.

Of course, a grandparent can also choose to establish a Trust for the benefit of the grandchild. This approach will offer greater flexibility than a 529 Plan (no limit on type of investment vehicle or use of finds), but will not have the 529 Plan's

111

tax benefits. (See Chapters 12 and 13 for Gift Tax issues relating to such Trusts.)

Estate Tax Benefits

Question 13 discusses the popular estate-planning technique of making annual gifts to reduce the Donor's Gross Estate at the time of his or her death. In addition to reducing the potential Estate Tax liability, the gifts shift income taxes attributable to the donated assets. In other words, if a grandfather and grandmother gave stock worth $20,000 to each of five grandchildren, the dividends earned from the stocks would no longer be taxed to the grandparents, but would be divided among the five grandchildren, who are presumably taxed at a lower income-tax rate. As a result, early gifting produces current tax savings on the income, while also reducing the Gross Estate of the surviving grandparent.

> *In addition to reducing the potential Estate Tax liability, the gifts shift income taxes attributable to the donated assets.*

Carryover vs Stepped-Up Basis

Key factors affecting a decision whether to gift an asset during lifetime, or to bequeath it at death, involve:

1. the difference between "carryover basis" and "stepped-up basis"

2. the imposition of Estate and Gift Taxes

The "basis" of an asset is the cost the asset is considered to have for tax purposes. The asset's cost comes into play when you sell it and have to determine whether you have gained or lost money from the sale. Basis is therefore sometimes referred to as the "tax cost" of an asset.

Determining as asset's basis can sometimes require careful record keeping. For example, if stock were originally purchased for $50, per share, and later split two for one, the basis of each share would be $25. Thus, if the stock were sold for $40, per share, the per share gain would be $15 ($40 minus $25). If the asset is subject to annual depreciation (such as an apartment building), the basis will be reduced each year by the amount of the depreciation deduction. Bookkeeping software like Quicken can help you keep track of such things.

Gifts During the Donor's Lifetime

When an asset is gifted, the basis of the asset in the Donee's hands will be the *lower* of (1) the same basis as the Donor had immediately prior to the gift; (2) or the fair market value of the gift.

Where the basis in the hands of the Donee is the same as the basis in the hands of the Donor, the basis is said to be "carried over." If the Donor paid Gift Tax on the gift, the basis would then be increased ("stepped-up") by the amount of Gift Tax paid. When the Donee sells the assets, the Donee pays taxes on any positive difference between what he or she sold it for and the basis of the assets.

An Example

Assume Mother, a widow, gives Son stock she bought for $3,000 in 1989. The stock is now worth $13,000. Mother's basis in the stock is $3,000.

Federal Gift Tax law allows you to give any person a gift of up to $12,000 in any one year without having to pay Gift Tax. Because the fair market value of Mother's gift is more than $12,000, she has to utilize $1,000 from her $1,000,000 lifetime Gift Tax Exemption ($13,000-$12,000 = $1,000; see Questions

12 and 13 for a fuller explanation). Son ultimately takes the stock with a basis of $3,000 (Mother's original basis).

If Son then sells the stock for $13,000 immediately after receiving the gift, the capital gain subject to income tax will be $10,000 ($13,000 minus $3,000). Because the son had to carryover his mother's original basis, he is allowed to add the time she held the stock to his holding period. Thus, even though he sold the stock immediately, he still gets the benefit of long-term capital gain because his holding period goes back to 1989.

Bequest after Death

Using the previous example, if, instead giving the stock to Son, Mother died and bequeathed it to him, the stock's basis would be "stepped-up" to the fair market value as of the date of death: $13,000.

In such event, Son could sell the stock and pay no income tax because his gain would be zero ($13,000 sales price minus $13,000 basis). However, the stock would also be included in Mother's Gross Estate at fair market value. Because the Estate Tax Rates are higher than the capital gain rates, Mother's holding the stock until death may result in higher taxes.

From this example, you can see that people who might be subject to the Estate Tax have a strong incentive to give money away now, assuming they can avoid Gift Tax.

Question 18

How Can I Safeguard My Affairs From My Own Mental or Physical Disability?

Expect the unexpected.
—Oscar Wilde

No one can predict the future. Good health and well-being are blessings we should enjoy while we have them. Most people make some arrangements for the financial security of the loved ones they will leave behind. But few people adequately plan for the possibility of a twilight period, when they are still alive but no longer able to look after themselves or their affairs.

This chapter will describe a number of precautions you can take to safeguard your and your family's interests.

Power of Attorney

A Power of Attorney is the authority given by one person ("Principal") to another person ("Attorney-in-Fact," or "Agent") to perform acts on behalf of and in the name of the Principal.

Although the person to whom the authority, or power, is given, is frequently referred to as an "Attorney-in-Fact," it does not mean that he or she needs to be a lawyer. For simplicity, we will use the term "Agent" to refer to the person to whom the authority, or power, is given.

Documentary Requirements

A Power of Attorney is created by a written instrument that designates the Agent and spells out, in detail, what powers and authority are given to the Agent. This instrument is signed by the Principal and is usually witnessed and notarized. As rules for executing Powers of Attorney vary from State to State, you should verify what your State of residence requires.

Limited vs General Powers of Attorney

A Power of Attorney may be "Limited" or may be "General." A Limited Power of Attorney restricts the Agent's authority to certain limited purposes, such as selling a specific piece of property. By contrast, a General Power of Attorney gives an Agent extremely broad and comprehensive powers to handle virtually every financial aspect of the Principal's affairs.

> *A Power of Attorney is signed by the Principal and is usually witnessed and notarized.*

A General Power of Attorney should comprehensively describe the scope of the Agent's authority. Before complying with an Agent's instructions, third persons will want to see the specific authority for the instructions in the document (that is, power to withdraw funds; power to purchase, lease, manage, or sell real estate; power to retain professional services; power to borrow money; power to buy and sell securities) before complying.

General Powers of Attorney need not give the Agent authority to engage in every possible transaction.

Legal Restrictions on General Powers of Attorney

The law does **not** permit an Agent to execute a Will on behalf of the Principal.

Also, an Agent may generally only make gifts (including gifts to himself) if the Power of Attorney gives the Agent specific authority to do so.

As discussed in prior Questions, there are several reasons for an Agent to authorize gifts to the Principal's spouse, children, and grandchildren. We recommend exercising great caution in selecting the Agent, but then giving that Agent authority to make gifts.

Durable Powers of Attorney

The Principal must be legally competent at the time he or she executes the Power of Attorney. Under English common law (which forms the basis for the laws of 49 of the 50 U.S. States), an Agent's authority under a Power of Attorney automatically ceases upon the Principal's incompetency. This rule creates a Catch-22, stripping the Agent of his authority when it is most needed. This dilemma was resolved through the adoption of "Durable" Power of Attorney statutes through the last 25 years; these statues specifically provide for a Durable Power of Attorney to continue in effect even if the Principal becomes legally incompetent.

Because the primary purpose of a Power of Attorney is to establish a procedure for the Agent to act on behalf of the Principal, who may be absent, ill, disabled, or incapacitated, future references to Powers of Attorney will mean Durable Powers unless otherwise specifically indicated.

Please note that even a Durable Power of Attorney will terminate upon the death of the Principal, because Probate laws transfer authority to act on behalf of an individual's Estate to Administrators or Executors/Personal Representatives.

Springing Powers of Attorney

The Power of Attorney can authorize the Agent to act:

1. at the time the document is properly executed by the Principal; or

2. upon some future event, such as when the Principal is determined to be disabled or incapacitated.

Type 2 is referred to as a "springing power" because it springs into effect upon the occurrence of a specified event (that is, the Principal's disability or incapacity).

Frequently, Principals capable of managing their daily financial affairs hesitate to authorize Agents to act unless absolutely necessary. Such Principals should execute Springing Powers of Attorney.

A Springing Power of Attorney must set out the criteria for the Agent's authority to become effective. Usually the triggering event is a determination by some trusted person that the Principal has become unable to handle his or her affairs on a regular basis because of physical and/or mental problems. This determination is usually made by a family member with the written concurrence of the Principal's treating physician.

Because the Agent will be required to deliver copies of the Power to banks, brokerage houses, title companies, and so on, notarized copies of the physician's written opinion confirming the Principal's disability must be attached to the Power when it is delivered to the financial institutions.

Please note that "disability" is not the same thing as "incapacity" or "incompetence." Someone who is aged or infirm may be "unable" to handle his on her business matters even though legally competent.

When a person in whom the Principal has complete trust (that is, spouse or adult child) is designated as the Agent, it is quite common to authorize the Agent to act from the inception, rather than use the springing power concept. As a result, the Agent need not worry about establishing the Principal's disability sometime in the future.

Indemnification of Persons Relying on the Power of Attorney

An Agent will often deal with persons at various financial institutions who know neither the Principal nor the Agent personally. Employees of these institutions may hesitate or refuse to handle the Principal's money in accordance with the Agent's instructions for fear the institution will be sued. The Power of Attorney should, therefore, contain specific language freeing third persons from any claims or liability in their dealings with the Agent.

Revocation

A legally competent Principal can always revoke a Power of Attorney. As a result, third persons dealing with the Agent may refuse to honor the Power of Attorney unless they can satisfy themselves the Principal has not revoked it. The Power of Attorney should therefore provide that the Principal must record any revocation in the office of the Recorder of Deeds for the County in which the Principal resided when the Power was executed. This provision enables a bank or institution, or any other third party, to treat the Power of Attorney as valid if a search at the Recorder of Deeds office turns up no revocation.

119

Combining a Power of Attorney and a Revocable Living Trust

Because all Powers of Attorney (including Durable Powers) automatically terminate upon the death of the Principal, an Agent can find himself or herself holding substantial assets, but lacking the power to do anything with them. Here, the Revocable Living Trust offers a practical solution.

At the time the Principal executes the Durable General Power of Attorney, he or she should also establish a Revocable Living Trust. The Principal can transfer his or her assets to the Trust right after it is executed, or can let the Agent effect the transfer at a later time (which must be prior to the Principal's death). The language in the Power of Attorney document must specifically authorize the Agent to transfer the Principal's assets into the Trust.

Taking the previously mentioned steps will achieve the following:

➲ The Principal can continue to manage his or her affairs while still able.

➲ In the event of the Principal's disability or incapacity, the Agent can take over the management of the Principal's affairs without the necessity of any court proceeding.

➲ Upon the Principal's death, Probate Proceedings will not interfere with management or distribution of these assets because they have already been transferred to the Trust, which continues to function after the Principal's death. Also, the transition will be facilitated if the Agent is named as the Trustee or Successor-Trustee of the Trust.

Question 19

How Do I Avoid Being Kept Alive on Machines if I am Comatose or Brain Dead?

It is not death, but dying, which is terrible.
—Henry Fielding
Amelia (1751)

Andy Warhol promised that each of us would have 15 minutes of fame, but none of us wants to earn it the way that Terri Schiavo did. Ms. Schiavo languished in a coma for 14 years while her husband and parents fought for control over her medical treatment.

Does anyone believe that either she, or her husband, or her parents, ever wanted the issue to be resolved this way?

Informed Consent

Over 90 years ago, Judge Benjamin Cardozo articulated the principle of "informed consent": "[e]very human being of adult years and sound mind has a right to determine what shall be done with his own body." This principle means that a

121

competent adult may reject medical treatment or procedures even if such rejection will hasten death.

Who Decides When the Patient Cannot, and on What Basis?

The principle of informed consent appears straightforward, but the Devil is in the details. What if the patient is not competent to make his or her own informed decision? How and by whom are such decisions to be made on behalf of comatose and incapacitated persons? These questions became the focal point of the 1976 Karen Ann Quinlan case.

Karen Ann Quinlan was a young woman, who was diagnosed as being in a persistent vegetative state without any cognitive functions. She was kept alive on a respirator. The key question became: "What decision would the patient have made if he or she had anticipated the tragic situation?" Her father was appointed as her legal guardian, and acting on her behalf, elected to have the respirator removed.

Missouri Limits the Guardian's Discretion Through a High Standard of Proof: The Nancy Cruzan Case

The Nancy Cruzan case involved a bitter fight between the parents of a young woman and the Missouri Department of Health. The patient, Nancy Cruzan, was in a persistent vegetative state, and was being kept alive with a respirator and feeding tube. The parents, who had been appointed as their daughter's surrogates, wanted the feeding tube removed, but the employees at the Missouri State Hospital refused.

The Missouri Supreme Court determined that any decision by the parents to withdraw life-sustaining systems must be based upon "clear and convincing" evidence that such decision was in accord with what their daughter would have intended. The Missouri Supreme Court found that because no such "clear and convincing" evidence was presented, the withdrawal of the life-support system was not permitted. The case was appealed to the U.S. Supreme Court, which held that Missouri's high standard of clear-and-convincing evidence did not violate Cruzan's federal constitutional rights.

The Florida Courts Have Their Say: The Terri Schiavo Case

The 2005 Terri Schiavo case once again illustrated how a different standard of proof can lead to a different result. Terri Schiavo's husband was appointed as her guardian. Because Florida did not impose the high clear-and-convincing-evidence standard applicable in Missouri, it was enough for her guardian to determine that had Terri been able to comprehend her condition and future quality of life, she would have elected to have the feeding tube withdrawn.

Terri Schiavo's parents fought this decision in the Florida and Federal courts for 14 years. Many readers will well remember the emotional impact the case had on the entire country.

The Simple Answer: Make Your Wishes Known

The above cases made for compelling television, but could have been avoided if the patients at the center of them had made their wishes known while they were still able.

Living Wills (Declarations of Intent) are Not Enough

Today, virtually every State provides for adults (usually over 18 years of age) to execute Declarations of Intent (often referred to as "Living Wills"). These documents state that in the event the signatory has an incurable and irreversible terminal illness without expectation of recovery and is incapable of making any healthcare decision, it is his or her intent that he or she not be kept alive by artificial means.

Usually, the patient's attending physician makes the determination as to the severity of the condition and the unlikelihood of any recovery. However, the person designated as the guardian, or surrogate of the patient must make the ultimate decision.

Because a Living Will is primarily an expression of intent, some healthcare providers (physicians, hospitals) may be reluctant to withhold, or terminate, certain life sustaining procedures without more explicit directions. For this reason, we believe *two additional documents should be prepared and executed* when the Living Will is signed:

1. a Healthcare Directive
2. a Durable Healthcare Power of Attorney

(See Appendix 1 for samples of all three documents.)

Healthcare Directive

A Healthcare Directive specifies the treatments and procedures that you do or do not want in the event you suffer an irreversible or incurable illness or injury and are therefore unable to make a healthcare decision.

The Directive should make your wishes known with regard to surgery or other invasive procedures; heart-lung resuscitation (CPR); antibiotics; dialysis; mechanical ventilator (respirator); and feeding tubes for food and water.

Directives usually state that the patient desires treatment to relieve pain and to provide comfort. You typically indicate which of the specific procedures are to be withheld by affixing your initials on the appropriate lines. Those procedures, or treatments, which are not rejected, will be administered.

Durable Healthcare Power of Attorney

The Durable Healthcare Power of Attorney may well be the most important document dealing with a "substituted judgment" for a patient's medical treatment. Durable Healthcare Powers of Attorney are far more comprehensive than are Living Wills. Living Wills only express your intent in certain limited situations; Durable Healthcare Powers of Attorney give broad discretionary powers for medical treatment beyond merely removal of life support and/or a feeding tube.

We discussed General Durable Powers of Attorney in Question 18, where we also explained the concept of a "Springing Power." A Durable Healthcare Power of Attorney combines two key elements to achieve its objective: (1) the Power remains valid notwithstanding the Principal's incapacity; and (2) the Agent's authority to make the critical medical decisions for the Principal *only* takes effect when the Principal is unable to make such decisions for himself or herself.

A Durable Healthcare Power of Attorney is *not* limited to situations involving irreversible or incurable terminal illnesses or injuries. In fact, the Power can be exercised by the Agent for the purpose of consenting to certain medical procedures to save the patient's life, or to treat a serious illness or injury. The persons designated as Agents are almost always the spouse, or adult children, of the Principal. Also, the Agent generally only exercises his or her Powers after obtaining the opinion of the patient's attending physician.

> *A Durable Healthcare Power of Attorney is* not *limited to situations involving irreversible or incurable terminal illnesses or injuries.*

Although it might seem logical to have the patient's physician designated as the Agent, many States prohibit this arrangement. Also, most physicians are prepared to give their opinion, but do not want the responsibility for making the ultimate decision.

The Potential Stumbling Block of Federal Medical-Privacy Law

The adoption in 1996 of the federal Health Insurance Portability and Accountability Act ("HIPAA") has made healthcare providers (physicians and hospitals) reluctant to release any medical information to a third person regarding a patient's medical condition. Notwithstanding the fact that a patient has executed all of the documents discussed previously, a healthcare provider might invoke HIPAA to refuse to furnish any information to the Agent. Without such information, the Agent cannot make an informed choice and therefore cannot act.

In order to avoid this impasse, we *strongly recommend* that all Durable Healthcare Powers of Attorney contain specific language whereby the Principal waives the privacy provisions of HIPAA and authorizes the release of medical information to the Agent.

Don't Rely on Family Consent Statutes

Because most persons do not have Living Wills, Healthcare Directives, or Durable Healthcare Powers of Attorney, some States have sought to alleviate the problem by adopting legislation referred to as Family Consent Statutes. These statutes provide, in essence, that if there are no documents signed by the patient who has been determined by a physician as being incapable of making his or her own medical decisions, a designated family member is authorized to act. However, rather than count on the State legislature to "draft" your documents, we recommend that you have an attorney properly prepare them.

Question 20

How Do I Find and Work With a Lawyer?

These are my lawyers...all Harvard men.
—Mobster Spats Columbo, in *Some Like It Hot*

No lawyer knows all the law, and most lawyers know only a little about those areas in which they do not practice. Just as medicine has become highly specialized, so has the practice of law.

If, as we hope, you decide to follow the advice in this book, you will need to find a lawyer who practices in the field of Wills and Estates. You will want someone experienced, honorable, and willing to work for a reasonable fee.

Word of Mouth

A satisfied client is the best advertisement for any professional. If you have used an attorney and were satisfied with the experience (personal services rendered, results achieved, and fees charged), that person should be your initial choice for a new assignment.

If Estate Planning is not that lawyer's primary practice area, he or she should be able to refer you to a specialist either within his own firm or at another firm. Next to doing the work themselves, lawyers like to refer work to other attorneys,

127

because it generates goodwill and the prospect of referrals in return. You should be aware, though, that some states permit fee splitting, which is when the lawyer who makes the referral gets a "cut" of the fee earned by the Estate Planning lawyer to whom he or she referred your matter. In a referral situation, you should always ask whether any fee splitting is going on, because it might affect the objectivity of a lawyer in referring you to the specialist who can best handle your matter.

If you are not personally familiar with a lawyer who specializes in Estate Planning, or who can refer you to one, you may have a relative, friend, or business associate who has had a favorable experience with such an attorney. If the person giving the recommendation is a person in whose judgment you have confidence, this may be a comfortable way to select an attorney to represent you. Among the most frequent sources of new business for Estate Planning lawyers are clients who were referred by other clients.

Bank or Trust Company

Assuming that you do not personally know an Estate Planning lawyer, nor do your family or friends, try contacting a bank or trust company for a recommendation. Because banks and trust companies are frequently named as Personal Representatives and Trustees in Wills and Trusts, they usually have considerable experience in dealing with attorneys in this area. The trust officers at these institutions are generally able to evaluate the skills of the many lawyers with whom they deal.

When most trust officers are asked for recommendations of qualified Estate Planning attorneys, they are reluctant to give just one name. Most often, they will furnish the names of a few lawyers with whom they have had frequent contact and in whom they have confidence. Also, if you have a particular problem or question, the trust officers may be aware of attorneys who have had actual knowledge and experience in the area.

You can then contact all, or some, of the attorneys whose names where furnished and arrange for personal interviews.

Local Law Schools

All accredited law schools teach courses in Wills, Trusts, and Estate Planning. In many law schools, these subjects are taught by practicing attorneys, who are specialists in their respective areas. They teach one or two courses per year, spending most of their time practicing their profession. The law-school's Website or administration office can tell you who teaches these courses.

You can be reasonably sure that whoever is teaching Property or Trusts/Estate Planning at a good law school is an expert who also knows others in the field. If those teaching are full-time faculty, you can ask them for a referral. If they are practicing attorneys who teach part-time, you can ask them to handle the work; if they cannot, or are too expensive, you can ask them for a referral.

Estate Planning Section of the Local Bar Association

Most local and state Bar Associations have organized themselves into several sections, or committees, each of which serves a different field. Because the legal practices of Estate Planning and Wills and Trusts have become recognized specialties, most Bar Associations have sections or committees in these areas. Consequently, their members consist of lawyers who specialize in the services you are seeking. If you were to contact the applicable local (City or County) or State Bar Association and request the names and addresses of the members of the Estate Planning and Trust and Estates committees, they will be pleased to furnish the list to you. However, it is very unlikely that the Association will give any recommendation as

129

to any individual or firm. Nor should you assume that leadership in the Bar Association equates to skill; sometimes people obtain these positions through persistent networking rather than reputation for excellence.

You should review the Bar Association list to see if you know, or know of, any of the particular committee members. With the names of those lawyers who practice in the specific area, you can interview some of the attorneys listed and be able to contact and decide the person you want to represent you.

The Importance of Personal Chemistry

The relationship between client and attorney is a very special one. The client must have complete confidence in the attorney's abilities, integrity, judgment, and concern for the client's interest. Because the client must often "bear his soul" and tell his most personal thoughts to the Estate Planning lawyer, a close rapport between the two is essential. Thus, after meeting with some, or all, of the lawyers who were recommended, you should be able to determine the one with whom you had the best personal chemistry.

The client must have complete confidence in the attorney's abilities, integrity, judgment, and concern for the client's interest.

Initial Meeting

A few lawyers are willing to meet with a prospective client for an initial "get to know you" interview without charge. Usually this type of interview does not get into specifics and rarely lasts more than 30 minutes. You should confirm this arrangement when you first call for an appointment. Even if the lawyer indicates that he or she will charge for the initial interview, the fee may be money well spent. You are dealing with the future security of your family, and it is very important that the person you choose to represent you in this matter is someone with whom you feel comfortable working.

Fees

Because the vast majority of attorneys practicing in the Estate Planning area use an hourly rate as the basis for their fees, you should discuss the fee with any attorney at the outset. Although the attorney should be able to quote an hourly rate, it may be difficult to give you a precise amount of the total fee in advance. Neither of you will know how many meetings will be held, the length of those meetings, the possible complexity of issues that may surface, and so on, all of which will impact the total fee. However, an experienced attorney should be able to give you a reasonable estimated range of the amount that he or she believes will cover the services to be rendered. The scope of the services to be rendered and the fee arrangement (amounts and payment terms) should be reduced to a written Engagement Letter prepared by the attorney and delivered to you. This will go a long way toward avoiding or reducing misunderstandings and surprises.

One thing that will help keep fees down is to give thought to the issues discussed in this book, not to second-guess your own lawyer, but to facilitate your conversations with him or her.

A Final Word

Each field of the law has its own attractions, challenges, and frustrations. We think it fair to say that no field touches people more closely or directly than Wills and Estates. And from our perspective, no professional pleasure is greater than helping people safeguard the finances and well-being of themselves and their loved ones.

It has, therefore, been a pleasure writing this book. We hope it will be of help to you and your family.

A ppendix

Sample Living Will and Related Documents

The following samples are for illustrative purposes only. Do not try to draft and execute such documents without the advice of an attorney licensed in your state of residence.

Appendix

DECLARATION
[LIVING WILL]

TO MY FAMILY, ATTORNEY IN FACT, PHYSICIAN, LAWYER, ANY
MEDICAL FACILITY IN WHOSE CARE I HAPPEN TO BE, AND ANY
INDIVIDUAL WHO MAY BECOME RESPONSIBLE FOR MY HEALTH
OR WELFARE:

If the time comes when I, _____, am no longer
able to take part in decisions for my own future, this statement, made while
I am of sound mind, shall serve as an expression of my wishes and desires.

I have the primary right to make my own decisions concerning treatment that might unduly prolong the dying process. By this declaration, I
express to my physician, family, and friends my intent.

If I should have a terminal condition, it is my desire that my dying not
be prolonged by administration of death-prolonging procedures. If my condition is terminal and I am unable to participate in decisions regarding my
medical treatment, I direct my attending physician to withhold or withdraw
medical procedures that merely prolong the dying process. For purposes of
interpreting this paragraph, the terms I have used shall be defined in the same
manner as those terms are defined in Chapter ____ of the ____ Revised
Statutes (the "Living Will Act").

In addition to the circumstances and directions I have described above,
it is my desire, and I direct that, life-sustaining treatment or life-sustaining
procedures not be administered to me if:

(a) I have a condition that is incurable or irreversible and, without the
administration of life—sustaining treatment or life-sustaining procedures is
expected to result in death within a relatively short time; or

(b) I am in a coma or persistent vegetative state which is reasonably
concluded to be irreversible.

With regard to the foregoing, I intend to include among the life-
sustaining procedures that may be withdrawn or withheld, the provision
of nutrition and hydration, whether by means of a nasogastric tube or tube
into the stomach, intestines, or veins, or by any other means.

With respect to all of the circumstances described in this Declaration, I ask that medication be mercifully administered to me to alleviate suffering, even though this may hasten the moment of my death.

I recognize that the directions contained in this Declaration go beyond those that are currently provided in the Living Will Act. It is my intent in executing this Declaration to direct the withholding or terminating of medical procedures in circumstances described in the Living Will Act as well as under circumstances described herein that are beyond those provided in the Living Will Act. Hence, this Declaration shall constitute clear and convincing evidence of my intent in all such circumstances.

This request is made after careful consideration. I hope you who care for me will feel morally bound to follow its mandate. This Declaration may appear to place a heavy responsibility upon you; however, I intend this statement to relieve you of that responsibility and to place it, instead, upon myself, reflecting my convictions.

Signed this _____ day of _____, 2006.

_____

_____

This Declarant is known to us, is eighteen (18) years of age or older, of sound mind, and voluntarily signed this document in our presence.

| Date | Witness |
| | Address |

| Date | Witness |
| | Address |

Appendix

REVOCATION PROVISION
[SIGN THIS PAGE ONLY AS AND WHEN YOU WISH YOU REVOKE THE DIRECTIVE]

I hereby revoke the above declaration.

_____

Date_____

Healthcare Treatment Directive

I, _____, make this Health Care Treatment Directive to exercise my right to determine the course of my health care and to provide clear and convincing proof of my treatment decisions when I lack the capacity to make or communicate my decisions and there is no realistic hope that I will regain such capacity.

1.   I direct all life-prolonging procedures be withheld or withdrawn when there is no hope of significant recovery and I have:

  - a terminal condition; or

  - a condition, disease or injury without reasonable expectation that I will regain an acceptable quality of life; or

  - substantial brain damage or brain disease which cannot be significantly reversed.

2.   When any of the above conditions exist, **I DO NOT WANT** the life-prolonging procedures which I have initialed below. (Any treatments not initialed may be administered to me.)

  - surgery or other invasive procedures   _____ initials

  - heart-lung resuscitation (CPR)   _____ initials

  - antibiotics   _____ initials

  - dialysis   _____ initials

  - mechanical ventilator (respirator)   _____ initials

  - tube feedings (food and water delivered through a tube in the vein, nose or stomach)*   _____ initials

*Note: Said direction relating to the delivery of water shall not be interpreted to disallow hydration by IV or other method to provide comfort or relieve suffering

3.   If my physician believes that a certain life-prolonging procedure or other healthcare treatment may provide me with comfort, relieve pain, or lead to a significant recovery, I direct my physician to try the treatment for a reasonable period of time. However, if such treatment proves to be ineffective, I direct the treatment be withdrawn even if so doing may shorten my life.

4. I direct I be given health care treatment to relieve pain or to provide comfort even if such treatment might shorten my life, suppress my appetite or my breathing, or be habit-forming.

5. If any part of this document is held to be unenforceable under law, I direct that all of the other provisions of the document shall remain in force and effect.

IN WITNESS THEREOF, I have executed this instrument on _____, 2006.

_____

The Declarant is personally known to me and I believe the Declarant to be of sound mind. I am eighteen (18) years of age or older, I am not related to the Declarant by blood or marriage. The Declarant has declared to me that the Declarant has willingly made and executed this instrument as the Declarant's free and voluntary act for the purposes herein expressed.

_____   _____
SIGNATURE OF FIRST WITNESS   SIGNATURE OF SECOND WITNESS
_____   _____
Address   Address
_____   _____
City, State, Zip Code   City, State, Zip Code

STATE OF _____)
) SS
COUNTY OF _____)

ON THIS _____ day of _____, 2006, before me personally appeared the Declarant, _____, to me known to be the person described in and who executed the foregoing instrument and Declarant acknowledged that Declarant executed the same as Declarant's free act and deed.

IN WITNESS THEREOF, I have hereunto set my hand and affixed my official seal in the County of _____, State of _____, the day and year first above written.

_____   _____
My Commission Expires: Notary Public

Appendix

DURABLE POWER OF ATTORNEY FOR HEALTH CARE

1.DESIGNATION OF HEALTHCARE AGENT

I, _____, hereby apppoint: _____
     (Principal)   (Attorney-in-fact's name)

_____

     (Address)

_____

     (Home Telephone)

as my attorney-in-fact (or Agent) to make health and personal care decisions for me as authorized in this document.

2. EFFECTIVE DATE AND DURABILITY

By this document, I intend to create a durable power of attorney effective upon, and only during any period of incapacity in which, in the opinion of my Agent and attending physician, I am unable to make or communicate a choice regarding a particular healthcare decision.

THIS IS A DURABLE POWER OF ATTORNEY, AND THE AUTHORITY OF MY ATTORNEY-IN-FACT SHALL NOT TERMINATE IF I BECOME DISABLED OR INCAPACITATED.

3. AGENT'S POWERS

I grant to my Agent full authority to make decisions for me regarding my health care. In exercising this authority, my Agent shall follow my desires as stated in this document or otherwise known to my Agent. In making any decision, my Agent shall attempt to discuss the proposed decision with me to determine my desires if I am able to communicate in any way. If my Agent cannot determine the choice I would want made, then my Agent shall make a choice for me based upon what my Agent believes to be in my best interests. My Agent's authority to interpret my desires is intended to be as broad as possible, except for any limitations I may state below. Accordingly, my Agent is authorized as follows:

A. I authorize any physician, healthcare professional, dentist, health plan, hospital, clinic, laboratory, pharmacy, or other covered healthcare provider, any insurance company and the Medical Information Bureau, Inc., or other healthcare clearinghouse that has provided treatment or services to me or that has paid for or is seeking payment from me for such services, to give, disclose, and release to my attorney-in-fact, without restriction, all of my individually identifiable health information and medical records regarding any past, present, or future medical or mental health condition.

1. The authority given to my attorney-in-fact shall supersede any prior agreement that I may have made with my healthcare providers to restrict access to or disclosure of my individually identifiable health information.

2. The authority given to my attorney-in-fact has no expiration date and shall expire only in the event that I revoke the authority in writing and deliver it to my healthcare provider.

In addition to the other powers granted by this document, I grant to my attorney-in-fact the power and authority to serve as my personal representative for all purposes of the Health Insurance Portability and Accountability Act of 1996, as amended from time to time, and its regulations ("HIPAA") during any time that my attorney-in-fact (hereinafter referred to in the subsequent clauses of this paragraph as my "HIPAA personal representative") is exercising authority under this document.

Pursuant to HIPAA, I specifically authorize my HIPAA personal representative to request, receive and review any information regarding my physical or mental health, including without limitation all HIPAA-protected health information, medical and hospital records; to execute on my behalf any authorizations, releases, or other documents that may be required in order to obtain this information and to consent to the disclosure of this information. I further authorize my HIPAA personal representative to execute on my behalf any documents necessary or desirable to implement the health care decisions that my HIPAA personal representative is authorized to make under this document.

By signing this document, I specifically empower and authorize my physician, hospital or health care provider to release any and all medical records to my HIPAA personal representative or to my representative's designee.

B. To consent, refuse, or withdraw consent to any and all types of medical care, treatment, surgical procedures, diagnostic procedures, medication, and the use of mechanical or other procedures that affect any bodily function, including (but not limited to) artificial respiration, nutritional support and hydration, and cardiopulmonary resuscitation;

C. To have access to medical records and information to the same extent that I am entitled to, including the right to disclose the contents to others;

D. To authorize my admission to or discharge (even against medical advice) from any hospital, nursing home, residential care, assisted living or similar facility or service;

E. To contract on my behalf for any healthcare related service or facility on my behalf, without my Agent incurring personal financial liability for such contracts;

F. To hire and fire medical, social service, and other support personnel responsible for my care;

G. To authorize, or refuse to authorize, any medication or procedure intended to relieve pain, even though such use may lead to physical damage, addiction, or hasten the moment of (but not intentionally cause) my death;

H. To take any other action necessary to do what I authorize here, including (but not limited to) granting any waiver or release from liability required by any hospital, physician, or other healthcare provider signing any documents relating to refusals of treatment or the leaving of a facility against medical advice, and pursuing any legal action in my name and at the expense of my estate to force compliance with my wishes as determined by my Agent, or to seek actual or punitive damages for the failure to comply.

4. STATEMENT OF DESIRES, SPECIAL PROVISIONS AND LIMITATIONS

A. I specifically direct my Agent to follow any healthcare declaration or "living will" executed by me. If my declaration or "living will" is not applicable with respect to any life-sustaining treatment, I do not want my life to be prolonged nor do I want life-sustaining treatment to be provided or continued if my Agent believes that burdens of the treatment outweigh the expected benefits. I want my Agent to consider the relief of suffering, the expense involved and the quality as well as the possible extension of my life in making decisions concerning life-sustaining treatment.

B. With respect to Nutrition and Hydration provided by means of a nasogastric tube or tube into the stomach, intestines, or veins, I wish to make clear that I intend to include these procedures among the "life-sustaining procedures" that may be withheld or withdrawn under the conditions given above.

5. SUCCESSORS

If my Agent named by me shall die, become legally disabled, resign, refuse to act, be unavailable, or (if any Agent is my spouse) be legally separated or divorced from me, I name the following (each to act alone and successively, in the order named) as successors to my Agent.

A. First Alternate Agent: _____
          Address:_____
          Telephone:_____
B. Second Alternate Agent: _____
          Address:_____
          Telephone:_____

6. PROTECTION OF THIRD PARTIES WHO RELY ON MY AGENT

No person who relies in good faith upon any representations by my Agent or Successor Agent shall be liable to me, my estate, my heirs or assigns, for recognizing the Agent's authority.

7. NOMINATION OF GUARDIAN

If it becomes necessary to appoint a guardian of my person for any reason, I nominate my Agent (or his or her successors) named above.

8. ADMINISTRATIVE PROVISIONS

A. I revoke any prior power of attorney for health care. I do not revoke any other durable power of attorney executed by me.

B. This power of attorney is intended to be valid in any jurisdiction in which it is presented.

C. My Agent shall not be entitled to compensation for services performed under this power of attorney, but he or she shall be entitled to reimbursement for all reasonable expenses incurred as a result of carrying out any provision of this durable power of attorney for health care.

D. The powers delegated under this durable power of attorney for health care are separable, so that the invalidity of one or more powers shall not affect any others.

BY SIGNING HERE I INDICATE THAT I UNDERSTAND THE CONTENTS OF THIS DOCUMENT AND THE EFFECT OF THIS GRANT OF POWERS TO MY AGENT.

I sign my name to this Durable Power of Attorney for Health Care on this _____ day of _____, 2006.

My current home address is:

Signature:

_____

Name: _____

WITNESS STATEMENT

I declare that the person who signed or acknowledged this document is personally known to me, that he/she signed or acknowledged this durable power of attorney in my presence, and that he/she appears to be of sound mind and under no duress, fraud, or undue influence. I am not the person appointed as agent by this document, nor am I the patient's health care provider nor an employee of the patient's healthcare provider. I further declare that I am not related to the principal by blood, marriage or adoption, and, to the best of my knowledge, I am not a creditor of the principal nor entitled to any part of his/her estate under a will now existing or by operation of law.

Witness No. 1
Signature _____
Date: _____
Witness No. 2
Signature _____
Date: _____
STATE OF _____   )
) SS
COUNTY OF _____   )

On this_____ day of _____, 2006, the said _____, known to me to be the person named in the foregoing instrument, personally appeared before me, a Notary Public, within and for the State and County aforesaid, and acknowledged that he/she freely and voluntarily executed the same for the purposes stated therein.

_____
My Commission Expires: Notary Public